Frontis and title page photos: **Jon G. Robinson**

AUTOMOTIVE
ATROCITIES!

THE CARS WE LOVE TO HATE

ERIC PETERS

MOTORBOOKS
INTERNATIONAL

First published in 2004 by Motorbooks International, an
imprint of MBI Publishing Company, Galtier Plaza, Suite 200,
380 Jackson Street, St. Paul, MN 55101-3885 USA

The information in this book is true and complete to the best
of our knowledge (with the exception of Billy in shipping, who
swears he invented the Pacer by combining a Go Kart and a
500-gallon aquarium). All recommendations are made without
any guarantee on the part of the author or Publisher, who also
disclaim any liability incurred in connection with the use of this
data or specific details. No cars were harmed during the making
of this book, although many of the vehicles had it coming.

We recognize that some words, model names and designations,
for example, mentioned herein are the property of the
trademark holder. Many of the trademark holders, if said model
names are mentioned in front of them, will suddenly point
behind you and shout, "Oh my god, look out!" and then
run away. We use the trademarks for identification purposes
only, because saying "Remember this piece of $#!+." doesn't
really narrow it down enough. This is not an official publication.

Motorbooks International titles are also available at discounts
in bulk quantity for industrial or sales-promotional use. For
details write to Special Sales Manager at Motorbooks
International Wholesalers & Distributors, Galtier Plaza, Suite
200, 380 Jackson Street, St. Paul, MN 55101-3885 USA.

ISBN: 0-7603-1787-9

On the front cover: AMC Pacer. *National Automotive
History Collection.*

Edited by Peter Bodensteiner, Lindsay Hitch and Scott Pearson
Designed by Rochelle Schultz, Mandy Iverson and Tom Heffron
Cover Illustration by Megan Mickelson

Printed in China

ACKNOWLEDGMENTS

Putting together any book is no easy task. Like being pregnant, it's not something you want to do alone. The quality of the finished product depends on the steadfast help, assistance, and just plain being-there of the people closest to you. Pulling together my thoughts and plugging away at this thing while juggling my weekly columns and wrasslin' with balky old machinery should have ended with me on some grimy street corner blabbering about the Illuminati Conspiracy—or at least with my carcass hooked to an angioplasty machine. Instead, thanks to the anchor of my wife Jill, the rages, the bottle, and institutionalization were kept at bay.

My parents, David and Berta, also deserve a mention. Without their early enthusiasm and encouragement for me as a young would-be ranter on all topics automotive, I'd probably be a lawyer, bald, and hypertensive—with a Mercedes 190 and a McMansion—instead of a full head of hair and an orange Trans-Am.

The "Toothless Hillbilly" (he knows who he is) should also get a nod (not to mention a new bridge) for providing an endless mine of country-speak nuggets used in this book and many columns over the years—as well as for being a motocrossing buddy who brings a beer cooler for the compound fractures and puncture wounds.

Don't say anything. *Just do it.*

Thanks also to the good folks at MBI Publishing Company and my editor, Peter Bodensteiner—who initiated the idea for this thing and without whom it would never have happened.

Martie Tyler and Fred Durant at Netscape and CompuServe and Tim Ito at America Online have also been great during this long, literary Bataan death march.

Thanks, guys.

And finally, encomiums and applause are due any person brave enough to put pencil to paper (or mouse to Cray Supercomputer) and poke into the dark future of automotive styling. Without the inevitable bad there'd be a lot less good. Risks are part of the territory—and they often pay off fabulously. Picasso probably didn't know what he was painting until he finished, either. The same is likely true of the best automotive designers and stylists. The bad must come along with the good. So here's to you.

Keep 'em coming!

CONTENTS

1

FAKE MUSCLE CARS
Embarrassing the Motor Gods

2 EGREGIOUS ECONOMY
14 Reasons Why Poverty Sucks

3 LOATHSOME LUXURY
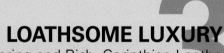
Badge-Engineering and Rich, Corinthian Leather

IT'S **MUCH TOO LATE** TO DUCT TAPE YOUR EYES

By the time you see an ugly car, it's already too late. The decisions have been made; the go-aheads given. *Millions* have been committed to a design that someone enthusiastically thought would be the next "in" thing—but which really should have been thrown in the trash, preferably after being used to wrap fish. Often, like the Nixon administration during Watergate, those responsible feel compelled to deny the obvious, hotly insisting that people will come around once they transcend convention and are able to appreciate the greatness in front of them. But like Nixon himself, in the end there's usually a shoe-shuffling admission of error (albeit with the *best* of intentions) followed by a fast-fade into oblivion.

And there's no such thing as "the elder statesman years" for a Gremlin.

This book is about vehicular Watergates—cars that scandalized standards of good taste and engineering, abused the public trust, and didn't rehabilitate themselves into a guest shot on *Miami Vice* like G. Gordon Liddy. These cars forever scar the landscape with their orange-peeling, rust-mottled, oil-burning, poorly conceived, and underpowered selves.

Some—like the iconic AMC Pacer—weren't all that bad and could have worked had their original design conception been followed. The Pacer was *supposed* to have been powered by a small, high-efficiency rotary engine rather than a conventional, heavy, fuel-thirsty piston engine. The whole car was built around this idea: its trademark width was intended to provide an extra-roomy interior and its chassis an extremely stable ride. But at the last minute the intended rotary engine that was to have been the very heart of the car was pulled, and a perfectly ordinary straight six was shoved in there instead. Now it was just a weird-looking car that was also heavy, slow, and conventional instead of a futuristic design that *might* have saved AMC.

Author Eric Peters. Yes, he owns a car with
a screaming chicken on the hood.

Others were simply unconscionable—even *actionable.* The self-immolating Ford Pinto of the early 1970s is the classic example; it was like a clown car, but full of Buddhist monks. Then-Ford President Lee Iacocca's single-minded determination to hold the little Pinto's weight to "not an ounce" more than 2,000 pounds resulted in a frighteningly vulnerable car with a back end too structurally weak to withstand being rear-ended by another vehicle traveling faster than 25 miles per hour. "Hit me—and we die together" became a popular Pinto bumper sticker (but many owners never put them on for fear of causing an explosion). During the subsequent litigation, it was revealed that it would have cost Ford a measly *$11 more per car* to reinforce the Pinto's rear-end sufficiently to handle a rear-end impact without igniting its occupants.

Others were bald-faced rip-offs—particularly the "badge-engineered" luxury car frauds of the late 1970s and 1980s. The low water mark here was that carbuncled automotive pustule, the Cadillac Cimarron—a gussied-up Chevy Cavalier—that sold for about twice the price. But there were plenty of others, too. In the name of making a fast buck, several automakers OJ'd their reputations and marketability almost beyond the point of no return. Cadillac is only *just* beginning to recover the prestige it once enjoyed—almost a quarter-century after the Cimarron debacle.

Then there were the simply depressing "all hat, no cattle" fake muscle cars of the 1970s and 1980s—the era when stripes and decal packages became the equivalent of Sponge Bob Squarepants' inflatable biceps, and just as full of hot air. Cosmetically as loud as their forebearers of the 1960s, the sulky heavy-breathers of the post–muscle car era *were* promising to look at. People saw the same "air induction" hood scoops, wild paint schemes, and aggressive stance that heralded a fast car prior to 1970. But they got an ugly surprise the first time they punched it after leaving the dealer's lot. Unless you were pointed downhill, few of the "muscle cars" built between 1974 and 1985 were capable of reaching 60 miles per hour from a standstill much quicker than a typical 2004 model-year compact with a four-cylinder engine, like a Dodge Neon or Honda Civic. Only a few could top 110 miles per hour, all out—a feat even the most meager 1990s-vintage Hyundai can easily manage.

The focus of the pages ahead is on a particularly awful epoch for the automobile industry—roughly 1975 to 1990—and the rotten fruit that fell from the tree during those regrettable years. There are some notorious notables that precede (or follow) but for concentrated automotive dreck, it's hard to find a landscape more strewn with styling gaffes and brain farts cast in sheet metal and injection-molded plastic.

—Eric Peters

PART ONE

FAKE
MUSCLE

CARS

EMBARRASSING THE MOTOR GODS

For smokers trying to quit, there's "the patch." It helps to ease the cravings and makes the tobacco fiend forget the heady pleasure of an unhealthy—but oh-so-satisfying—illicit puff. For the American car buyer, and in particular, the enthusiast car buyer, the fake muscle cars of the mid-1970s and 1980s were supposed to ease the withdrawal symptoms of losing the real thing, just like the patch.

It's hard to imagine the pre-catalytic converter world of 100 octane leaded premium—and factory-installed multiple carburetor set-ups. It was a time when nobody cared about safety, "crumple zones," gas mileage, or what was coming out of the tailpipe—other than the sweet, eye-watering smell of unburned hydrocarbons. Engineers like Pontiac's John Z. DeLorean (father of the GTO) and Chevy's Zora Arkus-Duntov (the man responsible for putting the "sting" in Sting Ray) were doing to cars what Hunter S. Thompson and Ken Kesey were doing to prose—creating strange new forms, wild things that were barely under control.

For a brief decade, from about 1964 (the year the GTO was born) to 1974 (when the last of the real muscle cars, the SD-455 Trans-Am was built), it was a free-for-all of gigantic V-8 engines, redline tires, Hurst mags, Ram Air scoops, hood tachs, and close-ratio four speeds. MPGs were as irrelevant as a UN report on global warming. Horsepower—in multiples of 100—was all that mattered. "Win on Sunday, sell on Monday" was the motto and zero-to-60 times sold cars. Woe to he who was slow.

But like all good things it couldn't last, and in 1970 Congress passed Senator Edmund Muskie's Clean Air Act—an Extinction Level Event for the hell-raising, tattooed, bicep-flexing muscle car. Leaded gas and hauling ass were out, "sensible" cars were in—mandated by the killjoys in Washington. The mechanical Velociraptors died, crushed under a giant legislative meteorite; scurrying rodents could now take over the world.

By 1975, high-horsepower V-8s had completely disappeared. Only one or two V-8s made more than 200 horsepower, SAE net—and most of these were installed in huge family sedans or station wagons like Pontiac's lumbering Gran Safari. Not a one of them featured any special high-performance parts; they were big—that was all.

But it was thought in some quarters that maintaining the *appearance* of performance—cars that looked fast, but which were in fact slower than George W. Bush showing up for National Guard duty—would be enough to keep the dollars rolling in. People would eventually forget that hood scoops actually used to scoop air, not just block the driver's forward view, and that the rear tires used to squeal when you hit the gas—not the engine.

The result was a series of sad-sack cars that humiliated themselves—and their owners—at stop lights all over the country. It would take the automakers nearly 20 years to recover from the Clean Air Act and figure out how to build "responsible" cars that were also respectably quick and anything close to fun to drive.

In between, they came up with these . . .

13

MUSTANG II, COBRA II and KING COBRA
1974–1978

By 1974, the muscle car frenzy of the 1960s had petered-out like an all-night kegger at sunrise. After a ten-year bender with 100-octane leaded premium and 330-horsepower Cobra Jet V-8 engines, Ford Motor Co. faced a harsh hangover of "catastrophic converters" and watered-down 87-octane unleaded that you had to stand in line all day to get. Reeling, wild-eyed, and increasingly desperate, Ford belched up the Pinto-sourced, "downsized" Mustang II—a car with all the kick of a watered-down Shirley Temple.

The "little jewel of a car," as then–Ford Chairman Lee Iacocca daringly called it, was emblematic of the era—a time of equally-downsized expectations and a sad harbinger of things to come.

In addition to being much less physically substantial than any previous Mustang (the 1974 model was almost 20 inches shorter and a good 400 pounds lighter than the 1973), it was also the first entirely performance-free ersatz Mustang. Initially no V-8 engine was even available—a depressing "first" for Ford's pony car. The only alternative to the 88-horsepower Pinto-derived rattletrap four-cylinder engine was a just slightly less pathetic 105-horsepower 2.8-liter "Cologne" V-6 sourced from Ford's European operations—along with a half-hearted "Mach 1" stripe package intended to remind buyers of better days.

It was thin gruel, however, compared to the previous year's fastback Boss 351—a car that would prove to be the last decent Mustang Ford would build for at least another decade.

In addition to being a shadow of its former self, the new Mustang's bodywork also tended to quickly develop the automotive equivalent of herpetic lesions in the form of angry-looking rust "sores" bubbling up over the fender wells that sprouted after just a year or two of exposure to the elements. Thin-gauge floorboards often rusted away within five years, leaving huge holes to stick your feet through to pedal the car, Flintstones-style—but without any noticeable speed boost. Automotive journalists of the era praised the Mustang II as being "right for the times"—even while noting that trim pieces often fell off in their hands, wheel covers would pop off in a hard turn, and performance was dismal even by economy car standards.

In 1975, Ford tried to re-attach some of the Mustang's gelded "equipment" by bringing back a V-8 option. But even though there were eight cylinders, just 122 horsepower was developed—an all-time low for the Ford 302—an engine that in "hi-po" form just ten years earlier had offered 271 horsepower.

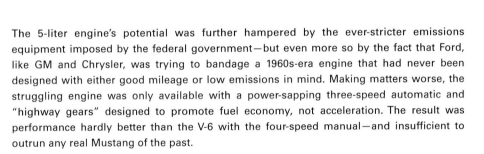

The 5-liter engine's potential was further hampered by the ever-stricter emissions equipment imposed by the federal government—but even more so by the fact that Ford, like GM and Chrysler, was trying to bandage a 1960s-era engine that had never been designed with either good mileage or low emissions in mind. Making matters worse, the struggling engine was only available with a power-sapping three-speed automatic and "highway gears" designed to promote fuel economy, not acceleration. The result was performance hardly better than the V-6 with the four-speed manual—and insufficient to outrun any real Mustang of the past.

Still, Ford gamely made a "performance package" of this basic combo—and in 1976 tacked on billboard-sized "Cobra II" stickers that screamed "I'm slow!" in perfect tune with the sickly whistle blowing from the single exhaust pipe. By 1977, an even more gaudy set of fiberglass air dams, chin spoilers, and a hood scoop that didn't scoop anything were added. It seemed the weaker the car got, the more aggressive and outsize the decals it was papered-over with.

The ultimate embarrassment came in 1978—when the blunt-toothed, sore-gummed King Cobra appeared. Taking a cue from the huge success of Pontiac's Trans-Am of the period, Ford may have reasoned that buyers would at least feel fast driving a car with a massive prismatic decal of a stylized Cobra draped over the hood and loud "5.0" engine call-outs on the now rear-facing—but still fake—hood scoop.

Five thousand King Cobras were made before the plug was mercifully pulled—and the damage to Mustang's once-proud legacy was finally put to an end.

In 1976, a Cobra II was featured in the popular TV show *Charlie's Angels* and driven by Farrah Fawcett's character, Jill Munroe. At least *she* looked good.

In 1974, 296,041 Mustang IIs were built—double the number manufactured in 1973. But production plummeted by 49 percent the following year.

1974 was the first year a four-cylinder engine was used in a Mustang—and the first year no V-8 option was even offered. (You want eight cylinders? Buy two cars!)

The downsized Mustang II was named "Car of the Year" by *Motor Trend* magazine in 1974—the same year that the song from The Towering Inferno won an Academy Award.

1977 was the first year for glass T-tops, which became a popular option—and the Cobra's fake hood scoop now had its "air intake" at the back (facing the windshield) rather than up front.

CHEVY CAMARO Z28

1977–1981

The smart athlete retires gracefully, at his peak—*before* he starts to slip and give off that "has-been" stink. To their credit, that's what Chevrolet managers did when they discontinued the Z28 version of the popular Camaro sport coupe after the 1974 model year. True high-performance engines—such as the 1970–1971 Z28's solid lifter-equipped, high-compression LT-1 V-8—had become all but impossible to build to socially-responsible specifications. So it was decided to allow the Z28 RPO (Regular Production Option) a dignified fade-away with its well-earned reputation still intact, rather than exploit the old car's performance image to sell new models that had none.

For two years—1975 and 1976—there was no Z28 option at all, conferring a sort of moral superiority on Chevrolet for not trying to slip the public a four-wheeled "roofie." Other brands (notably Ford and its Mustang II) had been shamelessly exploiting the legacy of their once-proud performance cars of the 1960s to hawk their enfeebled replacements. For a while, "Z28" still meant something on the street, unlike "Cobra," which by the mid-1970s had become synonymous with gutless stripe-and-decal disco cruisers driven by guys wearing medallions and too-tight Vidal Sassoon jeans.

It didn't last. After two years of resisting the same temptation that had gotten the better of Ford, Chevy brought back the Z28—but in name only, like "New Coke." The "all-new" 1977 Z28 did not have a special high-performance engine, as it had in years past. No 290-horsepower 302 with cross-ram carbs and cowl induction; not even the 1974's still-respectable L-82 with Corvette cam, decent cylinder heads, and 245 horsepower.

Instead, the 1977 Z28 was motivated by the same low-output, low-compression LM1 350 V-8 used in grandma-destined Malibus and Novas. It was, in fact, exactly the same engine used in non-Z28 1975 and 1976 Camaros—right down to the emissions-calibrated carburetor, cast-iron exhaust manifolds, and single exhaust. The 1977 "Z28" was nothing but a hasty skin job. It didn't even come with a fake hood scoop—just a decal that *suggested one.* Kind of like that spray-on stuff that suggests hair on a bald spot.

This same basic engine lasted through 1981—by which time Chevy had at least bolted on a fiberglass "air induction" hood scoop and fitted the flabby Z with 15x7-inch cast aluminum wheels instead of the heavy stamped steel Rally wheels that had been used in 1977 through 1979. In a bid to bleed away some sales from Pontiac's highly successful Trans-Am, Chevy also added a chin spoiler, fender flares, and dummy air extractors after 1978—features that did little to make the car any faster.

1979 Camaro Z28: From people who know what performance is all about.

On the track, and on TV, you've seen some of the best drivers in the world driving race-prepped Chevrolet Camaro Z28s in the International Race of Champions.

And maybe you imagined yourself behind the wheel.

For when it comes to hugging a road, a Z28 is truly something special. Not just any road, mind you, but the ones that twist and turn, sweep up and down. The roads that are the most demanding. They bring out the best in Z28. And we make sure we put our best into it.

We start with a special Z28 Sport suspension system. Then we add things like a 4-speed close-ratio manual transmission connected to an 11-inch high-capacity clutch. Front/rear stabilizer bars, special shocks, power steering, power brakes. To top it all off, we pack a 5.7 Litre (350 Cu. In.) 4-barrel V8 under the hood. (Camaro is equipped with GM-built engines produced by various divisions. See your dealer for details.)

Because a car of Z28's caliber should

Standard Camel vinyl interior with available auto. trans. and other available options.

look as good as it moves, we've given special attention to its appearance. You, and everybody else, will know a Z28 from the outside. It comes with a rear deck spoiler, new front air dam, bold accent striping, air louvers in the front fenders, sport mirrors, distinctive black finished grille, and more.

Inside, you'll find a special large-rim sport steering wheel, full foam bucket seats, tachometer, voltmeter, temperature gage, an electric clock, and more.

Now stop imagining yourself behind the wheel. Grab hold and take it from Chevrolet—people who know what performance is all about. Buy or lease a '79 Camaro Z28. Then go road hunting.

Aluminum wheels shown are available at extra cost. Available white-lettered tires are supplied by various manufacturers.

CAMARO. THE HUGGER. Chevrolet

A fairly aggressive 3.73 rear axle ratio was one of the few legitimate performance pieces the car was allowed, but with so little horsepower available, and so much weight—nearly two tons of it—the performance gear set only served to limit the Z28's top speed to barely more than 105 miles per hour at the edge of the gutless V-8's 5,000-rpm redline. This was 20 or 30 miles per hour less than in the Z28's heyday four or five years earlier.

As toothless as the 1977 to 1981 Z28s were, they began to look better in retrospect when the downsized "Third Generation" Camaros appeared in 1982. The 5.7-liter LM1 350—an engine you could at least work with by adding aftermarket speed parts—had been dropped entirely, replaced by an even smaller and weaker 5-liter 305 V-8 that in top "high output" form offered a meager 165 horsepower, 25 less than the 1981 Z28's 350 four-barrel engine.

These were dark and dismal years, and the Z28 never fully recovered, even though power and performance eventually came back in the mid-1990s. By then, however, it was too late to undo the damage of a decade's worth of dragging the Z28's memory through the mud. GM eventually cancelled the Camaro (and its corporate twin, the Pontiac Firebird) for good after the end of the 2002 model year.

Z28 is meant to turn you on. Styled to turn heads. And engineered for drivers who want to stay close to the road and emotionally separated from whatever the neighbors are driving. A difficult set of goals magnificently fulfilled, that's Z28.

Z28. PARTS AND PARCEL, And Z28 remains true to its distinguished lineage. Chevy engineers have long understood that a road car's reputation does

RARE ROAD MACHINERY. not-reside in straight-line acceleration alone. So the muscles in Z28 are not restricted to its engine compartment.

Toward your better understanding, we solicit your inspection of the highly honed and refined parts that continue to make up the parcel of this rare road machine, the Chevy Camaro Z28.

Chevrolet

1981 CHEVY CAMARO. THE HUGGER.

Byron Olsen Collection

Beginning with the 1979 model year, all Z28s were fitted with 85-mile-per-hour speedometers—a measure intended to discourage people from speeding. (It also gave the owner the possibility of burying the needle.)

Though Pontiac's Trans-Am had stopped using exposed metal bumpers years earlier, the Z28 did not get a flexible "Enduro" nosepiece and tail section until the 1978 model year—four years after the 'Bird. (Aerodynamics are important when you break that 50-mile-per-hour barrier.)

The 1977–1981 Camaro Z28 was the last Z28 (and the last Camaro) to have an interior design substantially different from the Firebird's, including different dashboard, instruments, door panels, center console, and seats.

Unlike the original 1967 Z28 and models through 1974, the 1977–1981 Z28s were mass produced—and used engines no different from those used in other Chevy vehicles. The 1977–1981 Z28s' standard 350 V-8 could be ordered as an option in other, non-Z28 Camaros—something that was never allowed with the 1967–1974 models.

The 1977–1981 Z28 did not come with mufflers; to enhance the illusion of performance, the cars were fitted with twin "resonators" (basically echo chambers) and a Y-pipe aft of the catalytic converter to provide an approximation of that rumbly V-8 muscle car sound.

PONTIAC TRANS-AM TURBO 4.9
1980–1981

In 1970, *Car and Driver* writers called the 335-horsepower, 10.75:1 compression Ram Air III 400 Trans-Am a "hard-muscled, lightning-reflexed commando of a car." By 1980, the Trans-Am was a washed-up, beer-gutted T-topped disco wagon—a bloated parody of performance days gone by, not unlike Sylvester Stallone in *Judge Dredd.*

1979 was arguably the last year for a good Trans-Am because it was the last year that Pontiac's own large-displacement V-8s were still available—in particular, the popular option code W72, a "T/A 6.6 liter" 400-ci V-8 available with four-speed manual transmissions only. Though not as fierce as the pre-emissions Pontiacs of the 1960s and early 1970s, the 400-equipped Trans-Am was still very much a legitimate muscle car, able to run the quarter-mile in the high 14-second range through the Hurst-shifted close-ratio four-speed gearbox. If you removed the catalytic converter, plugged up the EGR system, and cut open the block-off plate on the hood scoop, the car came alive like Prometheus unbound. It was illegal as hell, but you could do it with impunity because the basic hardware was still there.

But when the 1980 models rolled out, the venerable 400 that had been around since the 1967 model year was gone, replaced by an all-new "Turbo 301" 4.9-liter engine that sounded pretty good on paper—it was rated at 210 horsepower, just 10 less than the previous year's 220-horsepower 400. But it turned out to be one of the top five engines most likely to be used as a means of weighing down bodies of ex-Mafiosi sent to "sleep with the fishes"—right up there with the Cadillac HT4100, the V-8-6-4, and 5.7-liter converted diesel.

The new engine was as breathless as a black-lung coal miner due to small valves and restrictive intake ports; it absolutely refused to produce power no matter how furiously its owner abused the gas pedal. All he could do was stare at the three glowing idiot lights ("normal," "medium," and "heavy") on the off-center hood scoop Pontiac had installed to let him know when the turbocharger was trying to defibrillate the flat-line 301 to life. It took the car 10 seconds to heave itself to 60 miles per hour under ideal conditions—if the turbo was working right and the wind was at your back.

The final nail in the coffin was the fact that none of the many aftermarket high-performance goodies that had been developed over the years to beef up Pontiac V-8s—intake manifolds, exhaust headers, high-flow cylinder heads—fit the new 301, making modification for improved performance all but impossible. If you bought the car, you were stuck.

Both the 1980 and 1981 turbo Trans-Ams were not available with manual transmissions, either—further crippling an already helpless "performance car" that could be dispatched by a good 1972 Nova with a 350 two-barrel. It took a typical 1980 to 1981 turbo T/A 17 or more seemingly endless seconds to heave its 4,000 pounds of leaking T-tops and quick-to-peel metal flake decals through the quarter mile, like Marlon Brando slowly making his way to the craft services table. It was a low watermark for a car that just six years earlier could dip into the high 12s with a set of aftermarket headers, some tuning, and drag slicks. Top speed was barely over 110 miles per hour, with the turbocharged motor scuffling and struggling at its 4,500-rpm redline like a mangy dog about to be put down. All the race-derived aerodynamic aids that made the original 1970 Trans-Am a car to be reckoned with—including the three-piece chin spoiler, trunk lid "whale tail," and front fender air extractors—were useless gimmicks on this latter-day fatty, which could barely get going fast enough to make them of any use anyhow. It was like fitting winged slippers on a hippo.

Today, the legacy of the Trans-Am is that it has been voted the car "Most Likely to be Driven by a Guy with a Switchblade in his Sock."

The 1980 Trans-Am was the first American car since the 1962 F-85 Oldsmobile Jetfire to offer a factory-installed turbocharged V-8 engine.

1981 was the last year Pontiac built its own V-8 engine; 1982 and up Firebirds are powered by the same "GM corporate" (Chevrolet-built) V-8 engines as Chevy Camaros.

The Garrett Air Research turbo used on the 1980 to 1981 Trans-Ams was originally intended for smaller V-6 and four-cylinder engines; in actual use it rarely produced the claimed 9 pounds of boost—accounting for the car's disappointing performance.

The 1981 Trans-Am was the first Trans-Am to be fitted with a computer and an electronically controlled carburetor; both were added to lower emissions and improve drivability.

The original 1969 Trans-Am was never eligible to compete in the Sports Car Club of America (SCCA) race series for which it was named—because the Pontiac's 400-ci (6.6 liter) engine was larger than the 5-liter limit allowed by SCCA at the time.

PONTIAC ANNOUNCES: THE WORLD'S ONLY TURBOCHARGED V-8

Wouldn't you know Pontiac would offer the world's first turbo V-8 production cars of the '80s. That's right. Pontiac's 1980 Trans Am and Formula Firebird are the only two production cars now available with a turbocharged V-8 gas engine.

The result is breathtaking. You'll appreciate the turbo advantage of extra power available when you need it. And the way this engine moves smoothly into turbo boost. (Firebirds are equipped with GM-built engines produced by various divisions. See your dealer for details.)

The cars themselves are as extraordinary as the engine. Both the new Trans Am and the sleekly sophisticated Formula Firebird cut corners with quick ratio power steering. Both can tame roads with a special available handling package that includes four-wheel disc brakes and rally suspension. And both cars are controlled from a cockpit that features bucket seats, console shifter and rally gage instrumentation.

Put the world's only production turbocharged V-8 cars through their paces at your nearby Pontiac dealer's soon.

More Pontiac Excitement for the Great Ones

GM MARK OF EXCELLENCE

CAMARO "IRON DUKE"
1982–1983

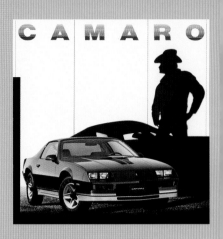

If you never want to get another speeding ticket, buy a used 1982 to 1983 Chevy Camaro equipped with the 90-horsepower "Iron Duke" four-cylinder engine and three-speed automatic transmission. Floor it and you'll age faster than the car accelerates. It took the 1982 Z28 nearly 18 seconds to cover the quarter-mile—with a "Cross Fire" V-8 engine under its hood. Now reflect on the possible forward momentum potential of the same basic car with *four fewer cylinders and roughly half the power.*

The 2.5-liter "Iron Duke" bears the shame of being the weakest engine Chevrolet ever installed in its Mustang-fighter. The look of the 1982 Camaro, with its steeply-raked front glass and compound curved hatchback, may have been "jet fighter inspired"—but the performance envelope was more like a grounded Cessna's. It was one of the few cars you could buy that approached the legendary leisure of the VW Westphalia Campwagon "hippie bus"—a machine that required 30 seconds to reach highway speeds and plenty of understanding from fellow motorists.

Luckily for GM, Ford had lobotomized the Mustang almost as effectively—leaving enthusiast drivers with a choice between slow and *slower.*

There were two engine upgrades available: a 2.8-liter V-6 rated at 112 horsepower, or the small-bore 5-liter V-8 with either a four-barrel carburetor (145 horsepower) or, at the pinnacle of power, "Crossfire Fuel Injection" and all of 165 horsepower. Even with the top engine, Camaro had lost almost 30 horsepower compared with the equivalent 1981 model—100, if you compared the 1981 Z28 350 with the 1982 "Iron Duke" 2.5 liter.

Luckily, the 1982 "third generation" Camaro was the most aerodynamic vehicle GM had built to date—which meant it picked up a little speed when going downhill. And after just a few years the four-cylinder was dropped and the formerly extra-cost 2.8-liter V-6 moved up to become the Camaro's standard power plant—ending the humiliation of being left in the dust by K-car station wagons.

The 1982 and up Camaros were the first Camaros to use full unibody construction with no bolt-on front subframe to hold the engine and front suspension, as had been the practice since the Camaro's launch back in 1967.

The hatchback body style of the 1982 Camaro featured the largest piece of compound curved exterior glass ever used on a GM production vehicle.

The 60-degree rake of the 1982 and up Camaro's windshield was the steepest of any GM production vehicle up to that point. It remains among the most aggressive windshield designs ever produced by any automaker. (If you can't be fast, at least look fast.)

1982 was the first year factory-installed fuel injection was used on a Camaro—but V-8s were still offered with a Rochester four-barrel carburetor through the 1986 model year.

A silver Camaro Z28 paced the Indy 500 in 1982—but the factory engine had to be pulled like a bad tooth and replaced with a custom-built Corvette power plant to enable the car to reach triple-digit speeds without the aid of a JATO rocket bolted to its roof.

SPORT COUPE

Interior shown in Maroon

Sport Coupe shown in Red

Sport Coupe could be the road car you've been waiting for. At a price you can afford.

Its modified MacPherson-strut front suspension, torque-arm rear suspension and radial ply tires give it an uncommon ability to hog the road. For the aficionado, the F41 Sport Suspension is available for tight, stiffer cornering.

A 2.5 Liter 4-cylinder engine with a new Electronic Fuel Injection system is standard. As are power steering and power brakes.

But that's just the beginning. Many, many more features—and the fun to go with 'em—are yours in Sport Coupe.

S T A N D A R D S

The standards you'll read about here combine to create the distinctive mystique that belongs to Camaro.

COLOR AND TRIM COMBINATIONS

Interior Colors

SPORT COUPE AND Z28 INTERIOR
- Vinyl Std
- Cloth Opt

BERLINETTA AND OPTIONAL CUSTOM INTERIOR FOR SPORT COUPE AND Z28
- Custom Vinyl
- Custom Cloth Opt

Z28—L/S CONTEUR DRIVER'S SEAT OPTION
- Cloth Std Interior
- Cloth Custom Interior

Exterior Colors
- WHITE
- SILVER (METALLIC)
- BLACK
- LIGHT BLUE (METALLIC)
- DARK BLUE (METALLIC)
- LIGHT JADE (METALLIC)
- DARK JADE (METALLIC)
- GOLD (METALLIC)
- DARK GOLD (METALLIC)
- RED
- MAROON (METALLIC)
- CHARCOAL (METALLIC)

SAFETY FEATURES

Occupant Protection
- Manual lap/shoulder belts with push button buckles for driver and right front passenger (driver's side includes warning system)
- Manual lap belts with push button buckles for rear passengers
- Energy-absorbing steering column
- Energy-absorbing front seat assembly
- Passenger guard door locks
- Safety door latches and hinges
- Folding seat back latches
- Energy-absorbing instrument panel and front seat back tops
- Laminated windshield/tempered side and rear glass
- Safety armrests
- Identification symbols for controls and displays

Accident Avoidance
- Side marker lights and reflectors
- Parking lamps that illuminate with headlamps
- Four-way hazard warning flasher
- Backup lights
- Lane-change feature of direction signal control
- Windshield defrosters, washer and dual speed wipers
- Vinyl-edged inside rearview mirror
- Outside rearview mirror
- Dual master cylinder brake system with warning light
- Starter safety switch

Anti-theft
- Audible anti-theft ignition key reminder
- Anti-theft steering column lock
- Inside hood release

Peter Bodensteiner Collection

Camaro's new possibilities are far-ranging. From expanded cargo space (shown above) that'll even take your skis. To its multi-position front bucket seats (shown far left). To the easy-to-view instrumentation and new console that holds its handy stowage compartment. Shown with available optional features.

Standard on all Camaros including Sport Coupe:
- Recessed quad rectangular headlamps
- Black flush-mounted windshield moldings
- Concealed wipers
- Sculptured body lines
- Lockable side stowage compartment
- Black glass and steel rear hatch
- 4-speed fully synchronized manual transmission
- Power steering
- Front-assisted front disc/rear drum brakes
- Delco Freedom II battery
- High Energy ignition system
- Front stabilizer bar
- Delcotron generator with built-in solid-state regulator
- Rear suspension with torque arm to handle driving and braking forces
- Rear suspension track bar for precise lateral axle control
- Triple-unit body construction
- Full unitized body construction
- Console with covered stowage compartment
- Carpeted floor, load floor, and stowage well
- Side window defoggers
- Day/night rearview mirror
- Black ignition and door keys

- 2.5 Liter 4-cylinder engine with Electronic Fuel Injection
- 195/75R-14 glass-belted radial ply tires (Shown above) optional full wheel covers and white stripe tires
- Black dual sport mirrors
- Square hub steering wheel
- Molded-foam headliner

- 2.8 Liter 2-Barrel V6 engine
- 205/70R-14 steel-belted radial ply tires
- 14 x 7 aluminum fin design wheels, gold-accented
- Body-color sport mirrors, left hand remote, right hand manual
- Square hub steering wheel
- Deluxe instrumentation, including tach
- Deluxe luggage compartment trim
- Electric quartz analog clock
- Specific smooth ride suspension system
- Custom interior trim and appointments
- Courtesy lamps
- Color-accented lower body with stripe
- Specific sound deadening materials
- Deluxe molded foam headliner

- 5.0 Liter 4-Barrel V8 engine
- 215/65R-15 steel-belted radial ply white letter tires
- 15 x 7, 5-spoke aluminum wheels
- Specific suspension system details
- Leather-wrapped steering wheel
- Full instrumentation including tachometer
- Specific black chrome exterior accents
- Front air dam and ground effect lower body extensions
- Special hood cowl induction
- Rear deck spoiler
- Dual resonators and tail pipes
- Body-color sport mirrors, left hand remote, right hand manual
- Color-accented lower body
- Molded foam headliner
- Courtesy lamps
- Electric quartz analog clock
- Specific front and rear bumper fascias

CAMARO POWER TEAMS

Engine	Ordering Code	Displacement (cubic inches)	Sport Coupe	Berlinetta	Z28	Manual	Automatic
2.5 Liter EFI† L4 (A)	L09	151	Std	NA	NA	Std	(1)
2.8 Liter 2-Bbl V6 (B)	LC1	173	EC	Std	NA	Std	NA
5.0 Liter 4-Bbl V8 (B)	LG4	305	EC	EC	Std	Std	EC
5.0 Liter CFI†† V8 (C)	LU5	305	NA	NA	EC	NA	EC
2.5 Liter EFI† L4 (A)	L09	151	Std	NA	NA	NA	EC
2.8 Liter 2-Bbl V6 (B)	LC1	173	EC	Std	NA	NA	EC
5.0 Liter 4-Bbl V8 (B)	LG4	305	EC	NA	NA	NA	Std

Std = Standard NA = Not Available EC = Extra Cost
* Floor-mounted shift control † Electronic Fuel Injection †† Cross-Fire Injection

Produced by GM
(A) Pontiac Motor Division, GM of Canada
(B) Chevrolet Motor Division
(C) Chevrolet Motor Division *NA Sport Coupe Berlinetta

COMPUTER COMMAND CONTROL. This sophisticated, thoroughly tested on-board computer continuously monitors gasoline engine functions and helps improve engine performance under all normal operating conditions, and the driver. An fuel mixtures are constantly adjusted to provide the system helps compensate for altitude, barometric pressure and temperature changes to help with fuel economy. Another benefit of Computer Command Control is that it is covered by the 5-year/50,000 mile emission system warranty. Ask your dealer for details.

23

A reeling and soon-to-be bankrupt Chrysler Corp. belched up one of the most pathetic paper-tiger muscle cars ever dreamed up in the form of the 1976 to 1980 Dodge Aspen R/T and the Aspen's sister car, the Plymouth Volaré Road Runner.

Tapped as the replacement for the aging Plymouth Valiant and Dodge Dart, the Aspen and Volaré would be among the last all-new designs to issue from Chrysler before the Big Crash came and the Age of the Minivan arrived.

Like their colleagues at Ford, desperate Chrysler product planners dredged up a couple of great nameplates from the company's salad days—the legendary Road and Track, or "R/T," designation for the Aspen; "Road Runner" for the Volaré—and glued 'em on cars whose only relationship to performance vehicles was the commonality of internal combustion—and even that connection was tenuous.

Under the hood of these stinkers was what Chrysler called a "time-tested" 318-ci V-8 that sucked air through a "lean burn" Carter two-barrel carburetor. The thinned-out air/fuel ratio—designed to keep emissions in check—made the otherwise decent workhorse engine notorious for hard-starting, stalling (often right in the middle of a busy intersection), and poor drivability. Tune-ups were necessary at every other fill-up, it seemed, because the cars just never ran right.

The Aspen R/T and Volaré Road Runner's performance was more dispiriting than their sheer awfulness as transportation devices—even by the standards of the mid-1970s, when the fastest sports cars were slower than most of today's V-6 family cars.

Pedal to the floor and wind at your back, the sad combo of a 318 V-8 and Torqueflite automatic delivered top speed comparable to a UPS delivery truck with a stuck throttle—about 108 miles per hour, flat out. Quarter-mile times were equally gimpy—a heaving 16.7 seconds at 85 miles per hour.

The final insult? *Every* 1976 and 1977 model was recalled for premature rust-through. Lee Iacocca himself later admitted the cars had been "rushed to market too soon."

It might have been better if they'd never made it at all.

An over-the-top "super coupe" variant of each car was offered in 1978; about 1,000 of these were built. These cars had a larger 360 V-8 with either 155 horsepower (two-barrel) or 160 horsepower (four-barrel). Super coupes had NASCAR-themed body kits, fender flares, louvered rear quarter windows, and wider wheels than regular Aspens and Volarés—but no significant mechanical upgrades. (WE CAN'T GIVE YOU WHAT YOU WANT, BUT WE CAN GIVE YOU SOMETHING THAT KIND OF LOOKS LIKE WHAT YOU WANT.)

Like most of the other strangled, would-be performance cars of the early catalytic converter years, there was no room for a true dual exhaust system on either the Aspen R/T or Volaré Road Runner—so all cars left the factory equipped with a restrictive single exhaust system that sapped even more vitality from an already-vitiated drivetrain.

YOU COULD STILL BUY HOLLOWED-OUT "TEST PIPES" TO REPLACE THE CATALYTIC CONVERTER AT AUTO PARTS STORES, THOUGH—THUS CREATING A NOISY CAR THAT WAS STILL SLOW AND ALSO SPEWED NOXIOUS POLLUTANTS INTO THE AIR.

DODGE ASPEN R/T
and PLYMOUTH VOLARÉ ROAD RUNNER

THE ASPEN AND VOLARÉ WERE REPLACED
IN 1981 BY THE SOON-TO-BE INFAMOUS
K-CARS AND THEIR DESCENDANTS, INCLUDING
THE CARAVAN AND VOYAGER MINIVANS.
(The K-cars were a clever ploy to make people
feel better about the Aspens and Volarés.)

THE "F-BODY" ASPEN AND VOLARÉ WERE AMONG
THE LAST REAR-DRIVE CHRYSLER PASSENGER CARS
BUILT BEFORE THE COMPANY WENT BANKRUPT
AND SWITCHED OVER TO THE FRONT-DRIVE ARIES
K-CAR IN 1981. MORE THAN A DECADE WOULD
SLIP BY BEFORE ANOTHER REAR-DRIVE COUPE—THE
VIPER—WOULD BE OFFERED.

ASPENS AND VOLARÉS SHARE IDENTICAL EXTERIOR
BODY PANELS; ONLY DIFFERENT GRILLES AND
TAILLIGHT TREATMENTS SEPARATE THE TWO CARS.
(Buyers had to go upmarket to a Chrysler Cordoba if they
wanted to get "rich Corinthian leather.")

25

CHEVY CORVETTE 305
"CALIFORNIA"
1980

The base price of the 1980 Corvette was $13,140; by 1981, this had risen by more than $3,000 to $16,258. More money got you less performance; par for the course in those bleak and ugly days.

Federal regulations required the installation of an 85-mile-per-hour speedometer in all 1980 cars, including Corvette, as a means of "discouraging speeding." (But the palsied engine was even more effective at inducing compliance with the double nickel.)

The 1980 305-equipped Vette was the first Corvette to be less powerful—and have a smaller engine—than a Camaro. (Chevy beat the Army to "Don't Ask, Don't Tell" by almost 20 years.)

A very popular option on 1980 Corvettes was the $391 Delco AM/FM stereo radio with CB radio. (Breaker, breaker. Anyone got their ears on? I'm keeping the hammer down, but I still can't pass anyone.)

The "Sting Ray" body style that was introduced in 1968 lasted all the way until 1982. Technically, there were no 1983 Corvettes. An all-new model appeared in 1984 featuring Crossfire Injection and 50-series Goodyear "Gatorback" tires—the largest tires ever installed up to that point on an American car.

The early 1980s were as unkind to the 'Vette as they were to cars in general, but California residents got singled out for special abuse. In order to comply with the stricter-than-national emissions control laws in effect in that state, Chevrolet was forced to pull the 5.7–liter, 350 four-barrel V-8 used in 49-state 'Vettes and substitute the "mini small block" 5-liter 305 V-8 to comply with regulatory edicts. Also snatched away was the possibility of a four-speed manual transmission; the LG4 305 "California Corvette" came only with a three-speed turbo-hydramatic—and a bad case of what Abe Lincoln once called "the slows."

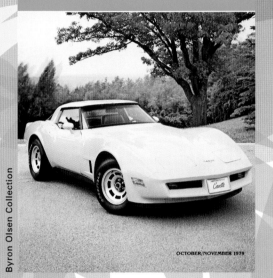

OCTOBER/NOVEMBER 1979

Since everywhere else in the country it was still possible to buy a four-speed, 350-powered Corvette with as much as 230 horsepower (if you chose the optional L-82 high-performance version of this engine), the 305/automatic California cars quickly became leprous outcasts among the faithful, and they remain so to this day. The small V-8 made only 180 horsepower—a little more than half the power of the 2004 Corvette's standard 5.7-liter 350-horsepower LS1 engine—and was smaller and less powerful than the less-prestigious 1980 Z28 Camaro's 190-horsepower 350 V-8.

Unusually lardy performance even by the dumbed-down standards of the early 1980s was the result of this engine swap—which rendered "America's Sports Car" little better than a flashy-looking "disco machine" that could barely even do a burnout on dry pavement—and only returned 14 to 15 miles per gallon as the final insult.

It was too much to take—even for the beaten down American enthusiast driver. Popular outcry resulted in a short, one-year-only run for the 305/automatic-only Corvette. The engine was discretely dropped in time for the 1981 model year, when the 350 V-8 was once again certified for use in California.

The bad news was that as the new model year dawned, the 230-horsepower L-82 option was gone, and 190 horsepower was all there was, take it or leave it. But at least buyers—including those in California—could once again specify a four-speed manual transmission and get the car to chirp the tires so as to impress the chicks down at the tiki lounge of their local Holiday Inn.

Like the family "funny uncle," the 1980 305 Corvettes are not talked about much by Corvette enthusiasts—and don't usually get much more than a let's-hope-no-one-notices footnote in official Corvette histories. About the only place you do find references to these cars is in Corvette value guides—which strongly urge potential owners to steer clear and point out that this model is one of the very few Corvettes likely to never appreciate significantly in value.

27

1983–1984 *HURST* OLDS
1985–1988 *442* OLDS

Oldsmobile had a long and distinguished history—and suffered a cruel and very public death. The process of mortification began in the early 1980s, when General Motors gutted the formerly independent engineering departments of each of its seven car divisions. Management eliminated the Buick-, Pontiac-, and Oldsmobile-built engines that had made each of these divisions' cars unique, not just "badge-engineered" clones of one basic model fitted with a different grille and set of wheel covers. Henceforth all divisions would share identical "corporate" engines built by a new entity, GM Powertrain.

Pontiac was the first to go; after 1981, it was no longer allowed to build its own V-8s and had to install Chevy-sourced engines in its cars, including the Firebird—which quickly became little better than a tarted-up Camaro. Pontiac ceased to be anything more than a hollowed-out marketing division for generic "GM" vehicles functionally identical to other GM cars.

Oldsmobile's trip to the glue factory began with the 1983 and 1984 Hurst Olds (and the similar 442 that ran from 1985 to 1988). Reaching back to the company's Great Days of the late 1960s and early 1970s, Olds product planners tried as best they could for one last hurrah before the ax fell—returning two well-respected muscle car designations to the lineup as an option group on the still-rear-drive (but not for long) G-body Cutlass coupe.

The 1983 and 1984 Hurst Olds looked OK from 20 yards; they had attractive black paint schemes with silver and red accents and were specially-equipped with an aftermarket-style Hurst "Lightning Rod" three-handled shifter: one stick for each forward gear. This was a bit much for a car with just 170 horsepower. But it was a good try, in very trying times. The little 307 V-8 wasn't much compared to the legitimate "455 Rocket" and "W31" high-performance engines of Oldsmobile's better days gone by, but it was at least an Oldsmobile-built engine, the last of its kind. Tied to 3.73 rear gears, it was still possible to do a decent burnout in a Hurst Olds or 442—if you power-braked the car or found a puddle to wet the tires a little.

From 1985 through 1987, the basic Hurst Olds package continued but was now called the "442," in reference to the 1960s-era Oldsmobile muscle car of the same name. Back then, the acronym was short for four-barrel carburetor, four on the floor (a manual transmission), and dual exhausts. The 1985 to 1987 442 did have a four-barrel carburetor, among the very last of GM's Rochester Quadrajets to be installed by the factory. But there was no manual transmission, the dual exhausts were as fake as Pamela Anderson's breasts (as a result of the single pellet-style GM catalytic converter), and the car's performance was as sickly as the Oldsmobile brand itself was becoming. Instead of the Hurst Lightning Rods, maybe it should have come with its own IV stand.

On the other hand, these cars began to look much better after Oldsmobile dumped the rear-drive G-body platform, switched over to front-wheel drive after 1987, and no longer offered the enthusiast buyer anything more meaty than a transversely-mounted 3-liter V-6 in a rebadged GM-generic Buick/Chevy/Pontiac/Olds clone-mobile—the "gutless" Cutlass.

Charles L. Gilchrist

In 1983, 3,001 Hurst Olds coupes were built—several hundred more than had been planned. Another 3,500 were made in 1984. These half-breed muscle cars are semi-collectible as representatives of the final death-wheeze of traditional, rear-drive/V-8 American performance coupes.

No other production car was ever offered with the Hurst "Lightning Rod" triple-tree shifter as a factory-installed option.

In 1984, the two-tone paint scheme was reversed; silver on top of black instead of black on silver. The absence of real performance remained.

The original 1968 Hurst Olds had a 390-horsepower 455 "rocket" V-8—almost double the output of the Hurst Olds' 307.

Four custom-built Hurst Olds were made in 1988—even though Olds had switched over to a new, front-drive platform for the Cutlass. These cars all had unique "Aero" rear window glass and "ground effects" body kits and were the last Hurst Olds models made. They were also the last rear-drive, V-8 coupes Oldsmobile would ever build.

1974 PONTIAC GTO

Craig George

Just as the last U.S. troops were packing up to flee what was left of the Republic of South Vietnam, General Motors' Pontiac division finally and fully abandoned the muscle car market it had almost single-handedly created ten years earlier with the introduction of the original 1964 GTO.

The 1974 GTO would have been an OK car—if it hadn't tried to be a GTO. Pontiac should have let the name fade out after the end of the 1973 model run, when the last semi-respectable GTO was built. It at least still offered a 250-horsepower 455 V-8 and had some street presence. Kind of like a 50-year-old *palooka* who might have been able to throw a punch, once upon a time—and might still be able to land a lucky right hook.

But the 1974 model was a mistake from the get-go. All the charisma and well-earned cachet of the GTO name was drizzled away in a single moment when the once-proud letters were affixed to a Ventura hatchback, a nothing-special compact that was itself little more than a rebadged Chevy Nova with a different grille and tail lights. The Nova/Ventura was by no means a bad car—but it was no GTO, and it showed.

Previously, GTOs had been based upon larger, more stylish Pontiacs such as the Tempest and Le Mans. These cars were attractive in their own right, even before being upgraded to GTOs. The 1974 Ventura, in contrast, was an obvious econo-box that would have been unappealing even if it had been fitted out with serious high-performance equipment. Of course, by 1974, with catalytic converters just a year away and truly powerful engines already gone, there was no high-performance equipment available in Pontiac's parts bin.

What squatted under the hood of the 1974 GTO was as nondescript and ordinary as its Chevy Nova–based exterior: a 5.7-liter 350 V-8 with a low 7.6:1 compression ratio and no specific performance parts to distinguish it from the engines in other ho-hum Pontiac passenger sedans. It

Craig George

was the smallest and least potent engine Pontiac ever put in a GTO. At just 200 SAE net horsepower, it had roughly half the peak power of earlier GTO engines, such as the 370-horsepower Ram Air IV 400 engine of 1970, and 50 horsepower less than the previous year's top engine, the 250-horsepower L75 455 V-8.

Pontiac made an attempt to transfer some of the luster of the still-capable Trans-Am (which could, if you had lots of money and connections, be ordered with a 290-horsepower SD-455 V-8) to the mini-sized GTO by fitting the Trans-Am's trademark rear-facing "shaker" hood scoop to the car, as well as a tachometer and floor shifter. But it was clearly an afterthought, and the little 350 V-8 didn't require great gulps of cool outside air like its distant Ram Air III and IV relations. All the scoop did was magnify the broken vacuum cleaner sounds echoing from the secondaries of the Rochester Quadrajet four-barrel carburetor, reminding the driver of all that had been lost and how little the GTO badge now meant.

As a general performance car, the 1974 GTO was just disappointing; as a GTO, it was an atrocity. The last of a proud line had been whittled away to a mere shadow of its former self, like an R-rated movie edited for commercial television. Buyers rejected it like a 300-pound blind date with braces and lederhosen. The GTO did not return for another engagement in 1975.

🐌 Unlike the 1974 Trans-Am, the 1974 GTO's shaker hood scoop *was* functional; a vacuum-actuated flapper door opened when the driver floored the gas pedal. The similar shaker scoop on the more powerful 1974 Trans-Am was blocked off—apparently due to federal "drive by" noise restrictions. The last year the Trans-Am's scoop actually scooped air was 1972.

🐌 The 1974 GTO, though the smallest and least powerful GTO, was not the slowest GTO ever built. Though few non-GTO people know about it, there was a "low performance" option available on the 1967 to 1969 models that delivered even worse performance. This model featured a low-compression 400 V-8 with a two-barrel carburetor and automatic transmission. This GTO was "for looks only"—like plastic food in a display case—and few people bought them.

🐌 The 1974 GTO shared many parts with the 1970 to 1981 Firebird, including a similar bolt-on front sub-frame that held the engine and front suspension. Since the car was light and simple, it made a good race car—once you removed the stock 350 and put in something with more beans, like an HO 455.

🐌 The 1974 model year was the only year a hatchback body style was available with the GTO package. (If it couldn't haul ass, at least it could haul lots of groceries.)

🐌 Though GTO sales after 1970 were poor, the lo-po 1974 "Goat" actually sold slightly better than the larger, more powerful 1973 Le Mans-based GTO: 7,058 units versus 4,806 units for 1973. But it was not enough to convince GM management that the car was worth keeping and the GTO option was dropped after this one-year-only run.

31

DELOREAN DMC-12
1981–1983

Benny D. Bosley

The DMC-12's gullwing doors require just 14 inches of clearance to open. Gravity, however, is not your friend when the gas-charged struts that hold them open begin to fail.

About 20 right-hand-drive versions were reportedly made for the export market.

No DMC-12 ever left the factory painted, but two gold-plated DMC-12s were produced, according to company records. (One is in a bank lobby in Snyder, Texas. The other was worn as a medallion by Vanilla Ice.)

While an engineer at Pontiac, John Z. DeLorean built the prototype for what would become the 1964 GTO at home, in his spare time.

DMC-12s have stabilized in value and most pricing guides put the current worth of a nicely preserved example in the $20,000 range—making it one of the few oddballs of the past that is appreciating in value rather than depreciating.

Despite a starring role in the hugely successful *Back to the Future* movies starring Michael J. Fox in the 1980s, John Z. DeLorean's futuristic DMC-12 gullwing coupe never quite took off. With just a 2.8-liter V-6 and a measly 130 horsepower, Doc would have had to put a lot of banana peels into "Mr. Fusion" to get the car to 60 miles per hour faster than the 10.5 seconds or so most magazines of the era were reporting. Top speed was listed at about 109 miles per hour—not very fast when being chased by irate Libyans, or even an angry Corolla.

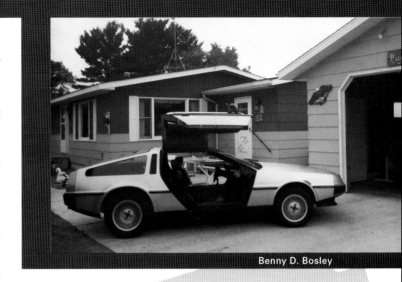
Benny D. Bosley

Why John Z.—a brilliant former General Motors engineer and solid "car guy" who helped father the original GTO while at Pontiac in the early 1960s—would expect a sports car as underpowered and overpriced as his DMC-12 to work is a question that has never been adequately answered. It is the classic example of wishful thinking and the perils of overconfidence. By the time the first cars rolled off the assembly line in Belfast, Northern Ireland, the projected retail price of a new DMC-12 had more than doubled, from an already expensive $12,000 to a ridiculous $28,000. That was *big* money in 1981, when $16,258 could buy a brand-new, fully-loaded 190-horsepower Corvette.

"I love my DeLorean—a truly fun car to drive, always turns heads, a car of unique design. In 1981 it was the car of the future."

—Benny D. Bosley

If the DMC-12 had offered exotic-level performance to go with its exotic-level price, things might have been different. But as it turned out, the DMC-12 wasn't even competitive as a performance car with the run-of-the-mill six-cylinder Camaros, Firebirds, and Mustangs of the era. It was simply too heavy—and its Renault-sourced small V-6 too weak. For all of its futuristic appearance, its performance was more like a trip down memory lane—to the Coolidge administration.

In its defense, the unpainted stainless steel bodywork designed by Giorgetto Giugiaro really stood out—and still does—*until it gets dirty*. Then it becomes as difficult to clean as the tilework in a Greyhound bus station. After just a few years of exposure to the elements, most DeLoreans assume the dull patina of old flatware in an abandoned hunting shack.

By 1983, the DeLorean Motor Co. was in receivership, and John Z. himself had been arrested (and videotaped *en flagrante*) on charges of money-laundering and conspiring to sell $24 million in cocaine as part of a bizarre scheme to raise investment capital via street junkies as a means of keeping his company afloat. His lawyers eventually saved him, but the car was doomed; just 8,583 DMC-12s were built before production was terminated.

Unlike the also attractive and "coulda-been" Studebaker Avanti—which has been revived a number of times by multiple companies since the demise of Studebaker itself almost 40 years ago—it's not likely the DMC-12 will ever be resurrected. The molds for the DMC-12's body panels were reportedly dumped somewhere deep in the Atlantic Ocean shortly after the company was dissolved, in an apparent effort to preemptively stamp out any future attempt at bringing the car back to the future.

33

Michael V. Mitchell

BRICKLIN SV1
1975–1976

BEFORE HE HELPED midwife the Yugo disaster in 1985, auto industry wheeler-dealer and importer Malcolm Bricklin tried his hand at building a car of his own. It's a tough call which idea was worse—the Bricklin SV1 "safety car" or the mid-1980s Yugo GV.

Like the later DeLorean—which shared some of its exterior styling cues, including most notably the upward-swinging gullwing doors—the SV1 coupe was supposed to be ahead of its time, a "car of the future." And in many respects, it was: Malcolm Bricklin incorporated energy-absorbing urethane bumpers and a tubular steel "safety cage" frame to protect the car's occupants years before these things became

The majority of SV1s (approximately 2,100) were powered by a Ford-sourced 351 V-8; the remaining 780 SV1s were motivated by an AMC-built 360 V-8.

commonplace features on mass-market cars. The body itself was a dent-resistant plastic material, very much like that of a modern Saturn. The colors—in the buyer's choice of Safety Red, Safety Green, Safety White, Safety Orange, or even Safety Subtan—were intended to make the car more visible to other drivers. Light scratches could be buffed out, and when the car's shine began to fade, all it took was a bit of polishing compound to bring it back. Repainting was never necessary.

Michael V. Mitchell

In theory, it all sounded fabulous. Many of the SV1's innovations—such as the plastic body panels—would be adopted by mainline automakers in the years to follow. But the SV1 was basically a kit car cobbled together using mish-mashed leftovers acquired from Ford and American Motors Corp. Lack of money and technical and engineering resources was evident in the way the car was put together. It had the look and feel of a teenage hot rod project built in the backyard with a Sawzall and some RTV. And though nominally a "sports car," the SV1 was heavy and slow. The 175-horsepower Ford V-8 engine used in almost all Bricklins (a few of the early cars had a much better 220-horsepower AMC-built 360 V-8) struggled under the load of nearly two tons of luridly-hued dead weight, the vehicular equivalent of Anna Nicole Smith.

The SV1, like the DeLorean, was also pricey: almost $10,000 for a car with performance inferior to that of a $5,000 car and which didn't offer the build quality of a $3,000 car (in mid-1970s dollars). Predictably, Bricklin's endeavor collapsed quickly and Malcolm Bricklin himself went on to other things, including a collaboration with Fiat that went about as well as the *Titanic's* maiden voyage—only to be followed-up in later years by the Yugo debacle.

If a Nuremberg-style tribunal is ever held for car designers and just plain bad ideas, Malcolm Bricklin will surely find himself in the docks to answer for his crimes.

Neither engine was available with a manual transmission—in keeping with the design philosophy of the era that a wheelchair operator shouldn't take risks.

BRICKLIN

The SV1 did not come with an ashtray or cigarette lighter at a time when these were common standards in other new cars and trucks. Malcolm Bricklin wanted to discourage smoking.

The SV1's twinned gullwing doors needed just 12 inches of clearance to open, which was touted as another of the car's safety features—unless one dropped on your fingers.

A contemporary road test of a 1975 Bricklin listed a 0-to-60 time of 9.9 seconds, a quarter-mile time of 17.8 seconds, and a top speed of 111 miles per hour—neck and neck with a new Hyundai Accent.

1987 **RENAULT ALLIANCE GTA**

THE DEATH RATTLE OF American Motors Corp. came in the early 1980s, with the "alliance" between the tubercular American automaker and France's largest automaker, Renault. Renault, a big player in Europe, hoped to gain access to AMC's fairly large U.S. dealer network; AMC for its part simply needed cash—*fast.* There was no money on hand to invest in new models, and without them, AMC was doomed. A marriage based on need rather than love produced the expected dysfunctional offspring—one of which was the "high-performance" GTA.

It's a measure of just how desperate times were for performance-car enthusiasts in the early 1980s that a loathsome little box equipped with a 2-liter, 95-horsepower four-cylinder engine could be marketed as "high-performance" and not incur a massive fine for false advertising or even criminal prosecution for fraud. But then again, by the skid-row low standards of the period, the GTA was in some respects better-than-average. The dulled masses were actually impressed by its 0-to-60 in 10 seconds—and its 17.5-second quarter-mile passes. Today, such a car would be considered on the borderline of dangerously slow. (A 2004 Dodge Neon SRT-4 reaches 60 miles per hour in just over 5 seconds.)

QUICK.

High-speed rated P195 .50VR15 Michelin® Sport XGT tires on 15 x 6 aluminum-alloy wheels.

2.0 litre high output overhead cam 4-cylinder engine with throttle-body electronic fuel injection.

Heavy-duty clutch with 4.07:1 per-formance axle ratio.

Tuned independent sport suspen-sion includes MacPherson struts and shocks, 24 millimeter front stabilizer bar and increased-rate springs.

Heavy-duty oversized front disc brakes with vented rotors, large calipers and double-acting brake boosters.

Venturing into sports sedan territory requires a car to live up to some very strict engineering standards. It has to handle pre-cisely and predictably. Reach desired speeds, *and* come to a stop, smoothly and safely. Reac-tions to driver input must be sure and, above all, *quick.*

Renault GTA meets these cri-teria, and then some. It's a car that instills you with a strong sense of confidence in its abili-ties from the very first turn. For some very good reasons.

Start with the powerful heart of GTA. . .a bored and stroked

GTA's standard close-ratio 5-speed gearbox shifts smoothly and quickly.

2.0 litre high-output overhead cam 4-cylinder engine with throttle-body electronic fuel injection that breathes freely through a low back-pressure, tuned exhaust system. Its power is satisfyingly steady—both silky-smooth and gutsy—and is trans-mitted to the road via a crisp, jewel-like 5-speed close-ratio gearbox and performance clutch, set up with a 4.07:1 axle ratio. This engine/transmission combination stomps out 114 foot-pounds of torque to make full, energetic use of every one of GTA's 95 horsepower, all the way up to its 6,000 rpm redline.

At the other end of the perfor-mance envelope is GTA's stopping ability. Its standard

power front disc/rear drum brakes with vented front rotors, large calipers and double-acting brake boosters act in concert to haul GTA down in a hurry. At the same time, they help keep brake fade and friction to an absolute minimum.

Also standard is taut power-assisted rack-and-pinion steering that keeps you in constant touch with what's going on underfoot, while maintaining an accurate "on-center" attitude.

GTA feels tightly locked down, yet light and maneu-verable at the same time. The tuned independent sport suspension is a big reason why. It includes gas-charged MacPherson struts and shocks, large diameter front and

stabilizer bars and increased-rate springs, all working through 15-inch aluminum-alloy wheels and sticky high-speed rated Michelin® XGT VR50 tires.

The result of all this serious equipment is nothing short of a driving and handling revelation: lateral acceleration numbers of .89 g's on the skidpad, outstand-ing transient response in the slalom, plus excellent straight-line acceleration. All helping make GTA's overall perfor-mance equal to, or better than, some

rear-wheel drive cars costing three to four times as much. Out on real-world roads, this trans-lates into an amazingly quick-feeling car that maintains an extremely stable driving profile in everything from the tightest corners to the smoothest super-highways.

Renault GTA. It's new and it's quick. Now turn the page and check out the hot!

RENAULT
GTA

Usually, front-wheel-drive cars do better in winter conditions, but *Consumer Reports* described the GTA as "one of the worst cars they'd ever driven" in the snow—due to its aggressive wheels and tire package, light weight, and low ground clearance.

All GTAs were factory-equipped with Ronal 15x6 alloy rims and Michelin XGT tires.

The 1987 GTA's base price was $9,000.

A few 1988 models may have been built, even though the AMC/Renault partnership had ended by then.

The car's name, "GTA," is derived from Renault's factory-sponsored racing cars—many of which were actually capable of busting a move.

Byron Olsen Collection

To be fair, the 1987 GTA actually handled well, generating skid pad numbers about as good as the Chevy Corvette that year. The problem was getting the car moving quickly enough to notice it could, in fact, corner decently. At a fast walk, even a shopping cart "handles" pretty well when you stop to think about it.

As fortune would have it, the GTA was one of the last vehicles to be produced under the weird AMC/Renault partnership before The End mercifully came in 1987. As if to call attention to the impending divorce, in its final year the GTA was stripped of all AMC badges and sold simply as the "Renault GTA."

After Renault abandoned ship, Chrysler Corp. took over what was left of AMC—mainly to acquire rights to the still-viable Jeep nameplate, which continues on to this day. AMC, on the other hand, has long since left the scene. Occasionally you'll see a rotting GTA sitting in the back row of a seedy used car lot—or serving as a makeshift chicken coop outside a trailer park. Appallingly poor quality control and susceptibility to rust have ensured that the few remaining operable GTAs won't be around much longer.

1982
RENAULT
FUEGO TURBO

An all-wheel-drive concept was considered but never produced. The added weight would have dropped the 0-to-60 time by at least another second or two.

The Fuego was offered with three different engines over its production run, ranging in size from 1.4 liters to 2.2 liters; none produced more than 110 horsepower.

Some things don't translate well—French-designed cars and Gérard Depardieu being perfect examples. The Fuego sports coupe was supposed to buck up the tottery AMC/Renault partnership; it was going to be the "image car" so desperately needed by a company beset by crashing sales and one design flop after another.

The ad copy said the Fuego boasted "racy good looks that can up the pulse rate on sight," though it may have more accurately described the heart flutters induced by the Fuego's frighteningly rapid depreciation rates. Running examples are almost worthless today—if, that is, you can find one that's still running. Most have long since been smelted into garden shears or put to some other useful purpose, such as building a barrier around Gérard Depardieu.

The car had an ungainly mollusk-like appearance—rounded in a way that reminded one of a slug struggling across the asphalt on a wet spring morning. The windows were too big, the wheels disproportionately small—and they were *metric*. As a result, only one specific type of tire could be used on the factory wheels, and many buyers found it was less expensive to simply replace the oddball metric-sized wheels and tires rather than pay the exorbitant price for the one-of-a kind Michelin metric tires specified by Renault.

Acceleration capability matched the Fuego's mollusk-like appearance; 0-to-60 took 10 seconds, assuming the peaky turbo was working, which it often wasn't. Top speed was barely into the triple digits—again, if all was functioning correctly (and the car was being chased with a dish of garlic butter sauce). Of course, other cars of the period were no great shakes in the acceleration department, either, but at least when *they* broke down it was fairly easy to secure the necessary parts—or find someone who knew how to duct tape them back together. But the Fuego, being French—and thus full of design eccentricities—was not only unreliable, it was often agonizingly difficult to find parts for, let alone a mechanic who knew how to fix one. The parts and service problem became much more acute when Renault fled the United States for good after the 1987 model year, leaving Fuego owners to figure it out for themselves.

The Fuego was front-wheel drive, but its engine was mounted longitudinally (front to rear) instead of transversely (side to side). This ate up a good bit of interior room, negating one of the front-drive layout's major advantages—and providing yet one more bit of evidence that the French make better cooks than engineers.

The Fuego remained in production in South America through 1993—long after production had ceased in France. Unfortunately, the Mossad never got to those responsible.

As recently as the late 1990s, used car value guides such as Kelley Blue Book listed the retail market value of *all Renaults*—not just the Fuego—at a flat $50, *regardless of year, model, miles, or condition.*

1975–1976

The DMC-12 gullwing coupe isn't the only bad idea that can be laid at the feet of poor old John Z. DeLorean. As Chevrolet Division Manager in the early 1970s, DeLorean had a brainstorm: He wanted to re-create the sales magic of the 1964 GTO—which he had personally helped design when he was chief engineer at Pontiac—but this time, using a compact economy car as the base vehicle.

He chose the Vega—a car that would become infamous as one of the all-time automotive stinkers ever to see the light of day—a lemon so tart it could make a Pinto pucker. The centerpiece of the awfulness was the Vega's engine—an all-aluminum four-cylinder that eventually became the focus of massive recalls. Aluminum is light and thus preferable to steel if the object is to shave weight. But aluminum is also a softer material than steel, so when it's used to make engine blocks, steel sleeves or inserts are typically used to prevent premature wear—and excessive oil consumption. But the Vega's 2-liter engine did not use steel liners; the pistons rode up and down in their aluminum bores, scouring out the soft metal—sometimes in just a few months of use—resulting in a smoke-spewing Exxon Valdez on wheels. DeLorean himself later admitted in his book, *On a Clear Day, You Can See General Motors,* that Chevy engineers "were ashamed of the engine," and that it looked "like it had been taken off a 1920 farm tractor." Of course, when a Vega was driving around, it often wasn't a clear day.

As for the car itself, DeLorean described the initial road test of the prototype at GM's Milford Proving Grounds: "After eight miles, the front of the Vega broke off. The front end of the car separated from the rest of the vehicle. It must have set a record for the shortest time for a new car to fall apart." Apparently the test was graded on a rather generous curve, however, and production continued.

This was to be the basis for the Cosworth Vega, a "high-performance version" of the Vega that Chevy hoped would "generate excitement and bolster interest in the GM small car market."

Instead it generated recalls and disappointment.

The aluminum engine was fitted with an innovative (for the time) four-valve twin-cam cylinder head, ostensibly to improve airflow and thus power output—but the added pressure only accelerated the disintegration of the already overstressed bottom end of the engine. "Firsts" such as electronic port fuel injection, the use of pressure cast aluminum wheels, and an exhaust header instead of a cast iron manifold weren't much solace to owners of broken-down, fast-to-crumble, and quickly worthless Vegas. Not even the partnership with well-respected Cosworth Engineering during the car's development made the Vega smell any better. Today it is regarded as one of the greatest performance car flops ever—a calamity of truly epochal proportions that haunted GM for decades to come.

The Vega model was finally cancelled after the 1977 model year. (American motor oil consumption plummeted. Oil company executives mourned.)

During the model's two years of production, 3,508 Cosworth Vegas were built—a much lower volume than had been anticipated.

In addition to the twin-cam 16-valve engine, all Cosworth Vegas featured special black paint with gold striping, gold-tinted instrument cluster facing, and a full gauge package with tachometer and sport-tuned suspension. The basic theme would reappear in 1976 on the 50th Anniversary "Smokey and the Bandit" Trans-Am.

The Cosworth Vega's 2-liter DOHC engine developed 110 horsepower, about 40 less than a typical modern economy car. (The 2004 Mitsubishi Lancer Evo has a 2-liter engine that produces 271 horsepower, more than twice as much as the Cosworth Vega.)

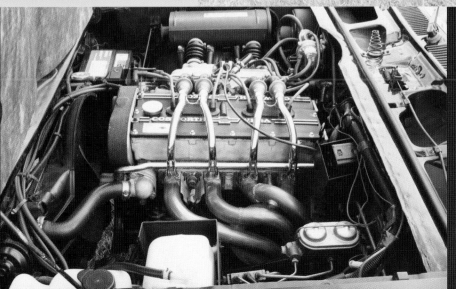

When new, the Cosworth Vega sold for about $6,000—perilously close to the cost of a new Pontiac Firebird Trans-Am or even a new Corvette.

43

Dishonorable Mentions

NOT a Martini Edition 924. You try to find one!

National Automotive History Collection

1977 Porsche 924 "Martini Edition"

The 924 series was originally designed under contract by Porsche for Volkswagen, which had planned to sell it under its own label. But when VW backed out of the project, Porsche bought the rights to the car it had designed for $60 million. Thus was born the "Poorsche," a Porsche for the impoverished. The car was powered by a 95-horsepower air-cooled four-cylinder VW engine—and didn't even come with rear disc brakes at first. It was basically a hopped-up Karmann Ghia. Despite regular upgrades—including the eventual installation of a turbocharger—the 924 remains one of the few Porsches that can be bitch-slapped by just about anything on the road with more than an angry hamster under the hood. Though the "Martini Edition" was named after a race series, a few hours in the car would definitely leave the dispirited driver in need of a drink.

1984 Pontiac Fiero 2M4

National Automotive History Collection

As with the Corvair almost thirty years before, GM's penchant for doing things on the cheap ruined what could have been a great car. The mid-engined Fiero 2M4 looked great and instantly became one of the sensations of the 1984 model year—until people realized those sexy, dent-resistant body panels hid Chevette running gear. Once again, GM tried to fix things after the fact—just as it had done with the "second generation" Corvair—by upgrading the Fiero's underpinnings and making a new 2.8-liter 130-horsepower V-6 and GT package available. But even a $100 million dollar investment couldn't save the car, and it was cancelled after the 1988 model year.

1979 AMC Spirit "AMX"

The sticker on the door was all this wretched Gremlin-based coupe had in common with the manly 390 AMX coupes of a decade earlier. Like other automakers at the time, AMC hoped to cash in on lingering fond memories of the old car to sell the new, even if the new one was an embarrassment compared with its ancestor. The 1979 "AMX" may hold the dubious honor of being powered by the weakest V-8 engine (on a per-liter-basis) made in the modern era. Despite having 304 cubic inches to work with, AMC engineers managed to wring just 125 horsepower out of the thing, about 45 percent of the output of the real AMX's 390 V-8.

National Automotive History Collection

The Citation X-11 was introduced in 1980, but no major changes were incorporated into the 1981 model.

1981 CHEVY CITATION X-11

With a name that might have been lifted from a 1950s pulp fiction comic book, Chevy's "performance" version of the front-wheel-drive Citation economy car gets no medals from enthusiast drivers. The X-11 package included "blackout" trim, Goodyear Eagle tires, a "sport" suspension package, decorative "cowl induction" hood scoop, and a "high output" version of GM's workhorse 2.8-liter V-6 that developed 135 horsepower. It had less power and was slower than most of the straight-six economy cars of ten years earlier, but it sold for roughly twice the price, about $6,800 when new.

1982 DODGE RAMPAGE

During the late 1970s and into the 1980s, fake fender-mounted air ducts and hood scoops became as trendy as the Village People and were festooned on cars just as tough. The 1982 Rampage and its Plymouth-badged cousin, the Scamp, were hybrid car/pick-ups based on the K-car platform. Each was equipped with the K-car's 84-horsepower 2.2-liter "Trans-Four" engine and offered performance to match. Buyers quickly saw through the scam and the Rampage/Scamp was discontinued after the 1984 model year.

1983 FORD ESCORT GT

Like a paid-for "date" found in a low-rent hotel's Yellow Pages, the Escort was not an automobile to drop your guard around or show off to your mom. In 1983, Ford put together a "sporty" GT version of the Escort with an 88-horsepower engine and all the regular model's plastic "chrome" taped over with flat black electrical tape, which was intended to make the car look like an hombre that could do some damage. Fog lights and different wheels were also added to give the car a more impressive, threatening look, but the effect was like sending out Siegfried and Roy in their capes and codpieces to stare down Tony Soprano. *Fuggetaboutit!*

Byron Olsen Collection

Above: Functional rear spoiler.

Standard GT Sport Performance bucket seats in Desert Tan cloth.

Display cars: Escort GT in Bright Bittersweet.

Standard GT instrument panel.

FORD ESCORT GT– IN SUPPORT OF THE PERFORMING ARTS.

47

1990–1993
Geo Storm

The Storm was more like a weak breeze, but that wouldn't fit on the fender. The Storm was a rebadged Isuzu Impulse sold through Chevrolet dealers, who figured an Isuzu-built car with a Chevy badge was likely to attract more buyers than a Chevy-built car with a Chevy badge. The Storm had a 1.6-liter 95-horsepower engine and delivered all the performance of a gut-shot muskrat struggling to escape from a dumpster. A "GSi" version could be ordered that upped the ante to 130 horsepower, and in this form it was fun to play with—the same way a Moped is. Just don't let your buddies catch you doing it.

Jon G. Robinson

X1/9
FIAT

X1/9

Innovative. Sleek. Striking. Far Advanced. Nuccio Bertone created the body. And he outdid himself. The X1/9. A brilliant performer. One reason is the mid-engine. A 1290 cc. inline 4, mounted transversely. Every major motor publication has reviewed the X1/9. And acclaimed it. The X1/9. Here's what Road Test says about it. "FIAT's X1/9 is a classic example of a sports car with the best possible configuration, maximum utilization of space, the best engine location for full performance potential, reasonable engine accessibility, good passenger accommodations and adequate luggage capacity—and it's all available at a reasonable price." We make the X1/9. And we couldn't have said it better.

Standard Equipment:

4 cyl single OHC engine · Weber carburetor/auto choke · Mid engine/transverse mounted · Vanity mirror · 4 wheel ind suspension · Expansion type cooling system · Cooling system electric fan · Rack & pinion steering · 4 wheel disc brakes · Dual brake system · Bucket seats/integral headrests · All vinyl interior · Removable roof panel · Integral roll bar · Safety door locks · Safety padded dash/visor · Safety screw type gas cap · Oil pressure/water temp gauges · Full carpeting · Catalytic muffler · Radial ply tires · Mag style wheels · Padded sports steering wheel · Energy absorbing bumpers · Left outside mirror · Day/night rear view mirror · Heater & defroster · Flow through ventilation · Electronic tachometer · Safety belts · Courtesy lights · Low fuel warning light · Emergency brake light · Hazard warning light · Retractable head lights · Steering column lock · 2 speed wipers w/washers · Cigarette lighter · Tinted glass · Electric rear window defroster

Specifications:

Body/Frame—Unitized construction. Reinforced longitudinal stress members. Two primer coats. Two coats of high-gloss acrylic enamel. Wheelbase 86.7" Front track 52.5" Rear track 52.9"
Engine—Mid. mounted transversely. S.O.H.C. inline 4. Water cooled. Vertical dual carburetor. Displacement 1290 cc (78.70 cu. in.) Compression ratio: 8.5 to 1. Bore and stroke: 86 mm × 55.5 mm (3.39 x 2 19"). Exhaust emission control system.
Clutch—Single dry plate.
Transmission—Four speeds forward plus reverse. Synchromesh in all four gears. Floor mounted stick shift in sports console.
Gear Ratios—1st. 3.583. 2nd. 2.235. 3rd. 1.454. 4th. 0.959. Reverse 3.714.
Final Drive Ratio—4.4 to 1.
Drive—Through the rear wheels by axle shafts connected to differential and to wheels through constant velocity ball joints.
Front Suspension—McPherson struts, lower lateral links and compliance struts, coil springs, tube shocks.
Rear Suspension—Chapman struts, wide lower A-arms and adjustable back links, coil springs, tube shocks.
Steering—Rack and pinion. Turns, lock to lock. 3.0. Turns in 32 ft. diameter.
Brakes—Large diameter disc brakes on all four wheels. Dual brake system. Mechanical parking brake.
Wheels and Tires—Self-ventilating steel disc wheels. Rim size d5Jx13" 145 HR×13 radial-ply tires.
Electrical—12-Volt system. 700-Watt Alternator. 60 Amp/hr battery.
Instrumentation—8000 rpm. electronic tachometer. 130-mph speedometer. Oil gauge with pressure warning light. water temperature gauge. fuel gauge with reserve supply indicator. battery charge indicator. Dual lighting switch and panel light switch are mounted on console. Dual spray nozzle and synchronous wiper operation.
Ventilation and Heating System—Provides windshield demisting and defrosting. Two air outlets mounted in console. Flow-through ventilation. Air intakes on cowl. Hot water heater. Regulators and two-speed heater fan controls mounted on console. Rear window defogger.
Fuel Tank—12.7 gallons.
Exterior Dimensions—Overall length: 158.5." Height: 46.1." Width: 61.8." Road clearance: 5.25."

FIAT
FIAT DISTRIBUTORS, INC.

The specifications on this sheet are given as general information and are not binding. Fiat reserves the right to effect at any time without prior notice, those alterations to parts, things and accessory equipment which they may deem necessary for any reason whatsoever.

PRINTED IN USA

1981 Fiat X1/9

Not everything that comes out of Italy—or the world-famous Bertone studios—is beautiful. Or fast. Or even nice. The country that gave us Ferrari, Sophia Lauren, and Bruno Magli also gave us Mussolini, the Mafia, and the Fiat X1/9. This mid-engined, targa-topped "poor man's Ferrari" delivered poor man's performance to match. With just 75 horsepower available, 0-to-60 sprints were more like casual strolls at 12 to 13 seconds. A "slow" Ferrari like the 308-series of the 1970s (the *Magnum PI* car) could make it to 60 miles per hour in about 6 seconds. Buyers responded in kind and Fiat was eventually "deported" from the North American market.

PART TWO

**EGREGIOUS
ECONOMY**

14 REASONS WHY POVERTY SUCKS

There is quiet dignity in the double-wide. Though the cinder blocks on which it sits may be cracking and askew, and while there may be nothing better than a stale box of half-eaten Cap'n Crunch and a warm liter of flat Mountain Dew for dinner—no one has to see your pain. Pull the duct tape–patched mummy bag tight, take another deep pull of "Night Train" wine, and wait until the missus gets home from 7-11 with that frozen turkey pot pie.

On the road, however, the world is a stage and all the people players—your station in life all-too-obviously conveyed by the rust-mottled wreck you pilot, the one that leaves a puddle of goo at every traffic light, backfiring like a mechanical colon as the light turns green.

Most of us at one point in our lives have owned a car we were less than proud of—and experienced the kind of self-abasement that finally motivated us to move out of Mom and Dad's place, find a job, and obtain the wherewithal to crawl up the automotive food chain a notch.

But every loutish college kid's $500 hooptie and deteriorating redneck lawn sculpture was once a brand-new showroom jewel that someone looked upon lovingly—maybe even took out a loan to buy. They did research; they read the reviews. And they chose . . . a Pinto Pony MPG. Or perhaps a Chevette diesel.

Honey, I'm home . . . come and see what I bought!

If ever social opprobrium were earned, it was by the people who spent perfectly good money to drive home in one of the following low points of automotive self-esteem.

CHEVY CHEVETTE
1976-1987

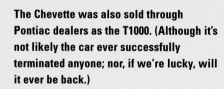

IT WASN'T MUCH, but one nice thing about Chevrolet's first attempt at designing a "world car" to compete on equal terms with the successful Japanese small cars of the mid-1970s was that if you put the transmission in neutral, revved the canker sore 52-horsepower engine to its redline and then dumped it into gear, the rear tires might spin for a few turns. That's because the Chevette was the very last of the few American-built subcompact economy cars to feature a conventional front engine and rear-wheel-drive layout, just like the larger cars of the time. This made for amusing, tail-out driving when it snowed. The car was ideal for shopping mall parking lot games of "chicken" and parking brake J-turns, inspiring a few enterprising hot rodders to remove the little four-cylinder engine and replace it with a V-6 or even a V-8, endowing the car with often-formidable—but always scary—straight-line acceleration capability.

Owners of Chevy's austere little econo-box could also casually mention their "'Vette" parked outside to comely (if gullible) prospects at singles bars—though it was critical that said prospects consume a minimum of three double-strong Long Island Iced Teas before suggesting a ride back to your parents' basement.

If you drove a Chevette when it was new, you were poor; if you got stuck with a used one as your high school ride, your parents were. But the car could help keep teen drivers out of trouble, especially the diesel-equipped version that was offered for two years.

The Chevette was also sold through Pontiac dealers as the T1000. (Although it's not likely the car ever successfully terminated anyone; nor, if we're lucky, will it ever be back.)

Initially, only a three-door hatchback was offered, but in 1978, a hatchback sedan appeared. Unlike the Pinto, though, a Chevette wagon was never produced.

The Chevette was heavily based on the 1974 Opel Kadett, a small car manufactured by General Motor's European subsidiary, Opel.

In the original pilot episode for the teen-angst show, *Beverly Hills 90210,* Brandon and Brenda are shown riding to their posh new high school in a Chevette, soon finding themselves parked amid a sea of sparkling BMWs and Mercedes. Brenda tells Brandon, "We need a raise in our allowance."

Darwin McGuire

Chevy literature and print advertising for the car claimed the Chevette would "Drive you happy." Or to the nearest street dealer for a fistful of 'ludes.

The 51-horsepower Isuzu-sourced 1.8-liter diesel affected the Chevette's already palsied ability in the same manner that a whack to Nancy Kerrigan's shinbone affected her ability to do a Flying Camel. Straining with all its might, the regular Chevette needed 17 seconds to drag itself to 60 miles per hour; the diesel option added another couple of seconds. Tickets were never a problem—unless they were for obstructing traffic.

Buyers with a need for speed weren't entirely forgotten, however. Chevy did put out a "High Output" version of the Chevette in 1978. It featured a 75-horsepower version of the now-standard 1.6-liter gasoline engine—enough power to qualify a Chevette as self-propelled machinery on most interstates and sufficient to achieve the heady 90-miles-per-hour terminal velocity necessary to launch the car over a couple of school buses at the local demolition derby.

For the last five years of its production run, the Chevette received almost no upgrades or improvements. It just sort of sat there like an old nag that just wouldn't die. The faux-'Vette was dispatched after the 1987 model year, replaced by the more modern, front-wheel-drive Cavalier as Chevy's number one bottom-feeder.

53

AMC PACER
1975–1980

Wayne's World immortalized the ungainly AMC Pacer, a car that defined the 1970s even more than a Bee Gees 8-track, the "Farrah" hairstyle, or the leisure suit. In fact, wearing a leisure suit and listening to a Bee Gees 8-track while driving a chiffon-yellow Pacer with wood panel accents to your job as assistant manager of the local McDonalds was perhaps the ultimate 1970s experience. You just had to be careful not to slide onto the optional "genuine Levi seat coverings" on a hot July day while wearing shorts; those "genuine" copper rivets that AMC thought were such a neat idea could leave burn marks on exposed flesh to rival anything endured by *Alias* Agent Sidney Bristow.

Richard Teague—AMC's vice president of styling—had intended great things for the Pacer. It had been planned as a thoroughly modern front-drive car. Power was to come from a highly efficient rotary engine (similar to the type found in the Mazda RX-8) tied into a compact FWD transaxle to save weight and allow for the maximization of interior space. With this layout, engineers could eliminate the need for a separate driveshaft and rear axle assembly; with no hump in the floorpan there would be room for three-across seating both front and rear. The Pacer holds the distinction of being the first mass-produced car to use the so-called "cab-forward" design later trumpeted by Chrysler Corp.

Unfortunately for Teague's grand vision and the Pacer's place in the automotive pantheon, when General Motors—which resource-depleted AMC had been counting on to supply the innovative rotary engines—abruptly dropped the project, AMC had to force-fit its own aged and completely conventional in-line six, an engine that dated to the 1950s, into the Pacer. As a result, the only thing "modern" or "innovative" about the car when it hit the showrooms was its unusual Humpty-Dumpty bodywork (supposedly, Teague was inspired by the aerodynamic shape of a football) and expansive exterior glass "greenhouse." In fact, nearly 40 percent of the Pacer's exterior surface was glass. This made for great visibility, but also let the sun bake the interior to infernal temperatures that caused early fissures and cracks in the injection-molded plastic dash—and also made it next to impossible for the over-taxed air conditioner (on cars that had it) to make the interior livable on summer days.

With no more than 125 horsepower on tap in its most potent form, the 3,500-pound Pacer didn't keep "pace" with very much, either.

Though it sold well at first—145,528 units in 1975—by 1980 that had tanked to just 405 coupes and 1,341 wagons.

It died quietly and unmourned the following year—although it has enjoyed a renaissance of sorts lately as the car most representative of 1970s design chic. As a car, it isn't much—but as a conversation piece, it's almost as good as having a restored "Elvis: Alive!" pinball machine in your den.

AMC advertising claimed: "You only ride like a Pacer if you're wide like a Pacer." (The entire ad department would later be tranquilized, tagged, and released in the Northwest Territories.)

The Pacer was built for just five years, with about 280,000 units produced, including a wagon version and the "sporty" Pacer X.

Randall AMC in Mesa, Arizona, built a handful of modified "Monster Pacers" fitted with a worked-over 6.6-liter 401-ci AMC V-8 engine in place of the standard 4.2-liter in-line six. The result was a fast, ugly car.

National Automotive History Collection

An unusual (and unique) Pacer design feature was that the passenger side door was four inches longer than the driver's side door.

Country Western singer Conway Twitty once owned a customized yellow Pacer with his initials stitched into the steering wheel. (In later years it was uncertain who was more embarrassed to admit this, Conway or the Pacer.)

People made fun of the Edsel—Ford's $400 million dollar mistake—but its resemblance to a chrome-splattered bus station urinal aside, at least the Edsel worked. Though hideous, you could count on the mechanicals underneath the skin, which were solidly Ford and thus as good as any other car of the era. The dreadful Yugo, on the other hand, was both hard to view on a full stomach and an out-and-out vile little car that stretched the most generous usage of such terms as "shoddy" and "slapped together."

This car was less reliable than the exchange rate of an African "People's Republic" or a Halliburton financial disclosure.

YUGO GV
1985–1991

When it was introduced to American buyers in 1985, the Yugo was touted as the least-expensive new car on the market, with an alluring manufacturer's suggested retail price (MSRP) of just $3,990. This was thousands less than competitor models from American and Japanese automakers. Unfortunately, it turned out the Yugo was anything but a bargain, teaching folks the hard way about getting what you pay for.

In this case, what buyers got was a really bad copy of an out-of-date Fiat whose engineering specifications seemed to have been scribbled on toilet paper after an all-night session of Stolichnaya shooters by the nogoodniks of Soviet Bloc Yugoslavian automaker Zavodi Crvena Zastava, which began manufacturing passenger vehicles for Soviet satellites in the mid-1950s.

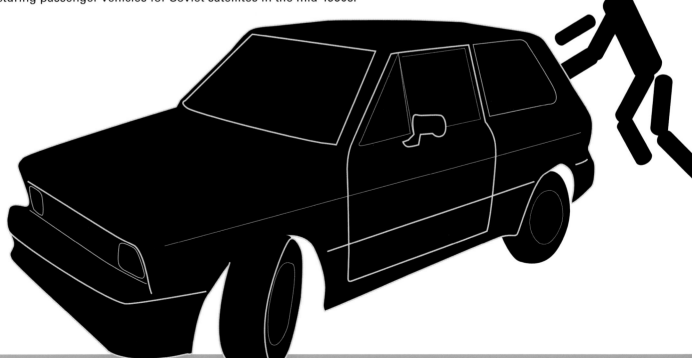

YUGO, $3990.*

EVERYBODY NEEDS A YUGO SOMETIME

*$3990 MFG. SUGG. PRICE FOR YUGO G.V. TRANS. $320, DEALER PREP. $90, TOTAL $4,400 EXCL. TAX AND TITLE.

Byron Olsen Collection

A Yugo derivative was marketed and sold in Italy; it was called the Innocienti. (Few buyers retained their innocence after the experience of owning one.)

In 1989, Yugo America filed for bankruptcy; a reorganization effort brought the car back for another two fitful seasons. A convertible model was briefly sold during the 1990–1991 model years—just before the company went down for the second and final time.

The Yugo was reportedly a "loose copy" of the Fiat 127; standard equipment included full carpeting, a cigarette lighter, an electric rear defroster, and a folding rear seat. Only the final 1991 models could be ordered with an automatic transmission.

A Yugo's reported top speed was 86 miles per hour at 5,250 rpm. A joke making the rounds in the 1980s went: How do you double the value of your new Yugo? Answer: Fill up the tank.

"Zavodi Crvena Zastava" roughly translates as "Red Flag Plant." (Which might have been helpful to buyers had they known beforehand.)

So long as the Iron Curtain held, Western buyers were safe. But as the political climate began to lighten up in the client states of the ossifying Soviet Union, auto-industry wheeler-dealer and ex-Subaru importer Malcolm Bricklin (already infamous for his SV1 "safety car") saw an opportunity to bring what he called a "simple, low-cost car" to the American marketplace. The parts about "simple" and "low cost" were true enough—but the same could be said of a 2x4 or a cinder block. Full disclosure should have included some other adjectives.

Initial demand for the cars was strong, and the 90 U.S. Yugo dealers that sprang up were accepting checks from people who had not yet even seen the cars, let alone driven one.

They should have waited.

The Yugo will likely hold in perpetual ignominy the title of "Worst Car Ever Sold to the American Public." Some broke down within a few miles of leaving the dealership lot—before the ink was even dry on the sales contract. A few were broken before they ever got off the truck; not many ran for very long without developing expensive, systemic problems ranging from premature engine failure to Superfund-level oil-burning. It wasn't so much a problem of defects plaguing the car as the car itself being a totality of defective engineering.

In 1999, during operations against Serbian strongman Slobodan Milosevic, NATO jets bombed the Zastava plant in the former Yugoslavia where Yugos were still being built. Unfortunately, the tooling for the cars was reportedly saved, and there's an ugly rumor floating around that Yugo—perhaps with help from Malcolm Bricklin—may make another attempt at bringing the precision engineering and build quality of an ex-Soviet republic back to the West.

Jon G. Robinson

VOLKSWAGEN
"THING"

1973–1974

The Bible tells us the poor are blessed in spirit—but they sure get short-changed when it comes to transportation. The Jeep-like VW Type 181 "Thing" didn't even come with carpeting. Like the old Beetle, its only source of heat in winter was the radiated fumes ducted into the all-metal, hose-out interior from the rear-mounted air-cooled (and oil-soaked) engine.

Ah, the scent of carbon monoxide in the morning!

Another endearing feature of the Thing was its cable-actuated clutch, which ran through a tube welded into the floorboard to the back of the vehicle, where the engine and transaxle were mounted. If not fastidiously maintained, the cable would eventually fray, snap, and slide back into the tube—where it was virtually impossible to fish it out without proper tools and plenty of time—leaving the driver to test his mettle at keeping the car going in whatever gear he happened to be in when the cable snapped. If you were lucky, the cable failed while you were in second gear; that gave you just enough speed to keep up with traffic without risking demolition of the 46-horsepower engine. You also had just enough leverage to get going again if you had to slow down for lights or traffic. If all you had was third or fourth, your clutch would die a quick and smelly death.

Jon G. Robinson

Volkswagen had wanted to use the name "Safari" for the U.S. market but could not do so because General Motors already owned the rights. Thus all Type 181s sold in the United States became "Things." VW's advertising slogan was: "Volkswagen presents the Thing. It can be anything!" (Except warm in the winter.)

Over its worldwide production run of approximately seven years from 1973 to 1980, some 74,000 to 140,000 Things were produced. Not even VW is sure of the exact number.

The Thing can trace its roots back to the World War II Kubelwagen—a light-armored personnel carrier that saw service with Rommel's famed Afrika Korps. The Schwimmwagen variant was designed to negotiate small streams. (The lesser-known Schnitzelwagen was a mobile snack kiosk.)

A car that goes just about anywhere.

Use it on the beach, dune buggy style. Take the doors off, take the windows out, fold the windshield down, fold the backseats down (and load up your gear), lower the top and let the sunshine in. If it rains, don't worry. Water drains out. Seats dry out without mildewing. And to help you get in and out of the dunes, its air-cooled engine is mounted over the drive wheels for better traction. Leave it to Volkswagen to help you make a good thing even better.

Mexican models—which were sold as "Safaris"—have a modified engine with an ultra-low 6.8:1 compression ratio to accommodate poor-quality gasoline from Pemex (the Mexican state–owned company). In the United Kingdom, the Thing was sold with right-hand drive and called the "Trekker."

At last, a car that can be anything.

Good for fun and good for work. Good for the city and good for the country. Good off-the-road and good on-the-road. For the shopping, the chauffering, the hauling—all the things you need a good passenger car for. The "Thing" parks like the Beetle. (It has the same suspension and quick responsive steering. Averages 21 miles per gallon. And it has the 24/24 Warranty (see specifications on back cover) like all Volkswagens. It's "The Thing"—the car that can be anything.

The MSRP for a 1973 Thing was $2,750; an AM radio with single dash-mounted speaker cost $64 extra. The Thing had no carpet or soft interior trim. An auxiliary gas heater was a popular option to help cope with the draftiness of the poorly sealed and insulated cabin.

A car ready to take on almost anything.

Ready to take the bumps, the lumps, the rocks and the ruts. It's got a high ground clearance. A platinum frame that shields the underparts from flying stones and debris. A four-wheel independent suspension so that each wheel takes bumps separately. And a double-jointed rear axle that makes the rear wheels hug the ground. It's a car built tough, but isn't tough to drive. For a small car, it's a heavyweight.

60

Byron Olsen Collection

On the upside, the Thing was said to be capable of floating (provided it had solid, non-rusted floor boards), just like its Type 166 Schwimmwagen World War II ancestor, and could be hand-stripped of its bolt-on doors, windshield glass, and roof (hard or soft tops were available) in a matter of minutes. This helped lighten the vehicle somewhat, reducing by a few clicks the 22.5 seconds necessary to run the quarter mile and the 23.2 seconds needed to reach 60 miles per hour. It also provided some cool air during the hot summer months. Unfortunately for VW and Thing aficionados, these same kit-car qualities also meant the vehicle could not pass muster under 1975 passenger car crash test standards in the United States, ending U.S. Thing sales after just two short years on the market.

A devoted following continues to keep these cars alive, however—almost 30 years after the last new one was sold. They are popular as backwoods knockabouts and are well-suited for carting around wet Labrador Retrievers. Best of all, the Thing is one of those great "who cares?" cars you can bump into trees without remorse. Three strong men can roll one on its back like a giant box turtle. Paint one in the authentic sand-gray camouflage of Rommel's Afrika Korps—complete with palm trees on the door and staff flag on the fender. Hum a few bars of "Deutschland, über alles!" as you motor along in the left lane—oblivious to the angry conga line of cars stuck behind you.

Son, it don't get no better'n this!

Dan Perry

Jon G. Robinson

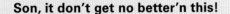

DO NOT DRIVE ON PUBLIC ROADS WITH DOORS OFF AND/OR WINDSHIELD DOWN. — SEE OWNER'S MANUAL —

AMC GREMLIN
1970–1978

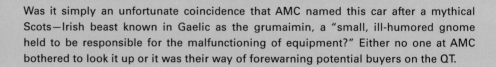

Introducing Gremlin GT

If you want it any racier, paint a number on the door.

The AMC Gremlin has always been a sporty, fun-to-drive car. But now we've got a snappy new version that's as racy looking as anything this side of a racetrack.

From the pinstriped front air dam right back to pinstriped rear fender flares, the new Gremlin X says, "Take me to your highway," loud and clear.

It has color keyed fender flares and front air dam, GT spoke-styled wheels with trim rings, DR 70 x 14 outline-white-letter steel belted radial tires, front sway bar, GT bodyside stripe, body-color bumpers with bumper guards and netting strips, dual black mirrors, and much more—all standard. Gremlin GT has plenty of indoor

sportiness, too. Standard features include a brushed aluminum instrument panel with rally instrumentation and tachometer, soft-feel vinyl bucket seats, sport steering wheel and extra-quiet insulation, to name a few.

Take the exciting new Gremlin GT for a test drive at your AMC Dealer's today. After that, you'll want to take it everywhere you go!

AMC

Why is it when the other car companies come out with sporty little cars, the cars come out looking the same?

There is an approach to the sporty little car that goes beyond the exaggerated paint job. And the Gremlin X is the first little car to take it.

It is, basically and fundamentally, the first little car to break with the design traditions of Detroit.

There is no traditional gentle sloping of the rear.

There are none of the conventional curves around the front and sides.

And there is no attempt to suggest more performance than there actually is.

Instead of a fat black stripe down the hood, there are real fat tires. Fatter standard tires than the Vega GT, Pinto Rallye, Maverick Grabber, or Comet GT offer you.

There are 4 of the new slot-style wheels and 2 bucket seats. The same bucket seats we put in our Javelin.

And instead of non-functioning hood scoops, there is a standard 6-cylinder engine that develops 135 horsepower. More cylinders than Pinto and Vega. And more horsepower than all four. Even the Gremlin X's optional engine

is a larger 6 cylinder than those offered by Comet or Grabber. It is 258 cubic inches and generates 150 horsepower.

But no matter how sporty the Gremlin X gets, it is still the original American subcompact. With all the economy and maneuverability that implies.

It gives you up to 25 miles to the gallon. And it is heavier, with wider front and rear tracks than any of the other four.

Finally, the Gremlin X lists for only $2299.* Which is quite a bargain when you consider what you're getting for your money.

Either a different-looking subcompact with the spirit of a sporty car. Or a different-looking sporty car with the advantages of a subcompact.

If you had to compete with GM, Ford and Chrysler, what would you do?

American Motors Gremlin X

*MANUFACTURER'S SUGGESTED RETAIL PRICE. FEDERAL TAXES INCLUDED. SEATS AND LOCAL TAXES, IF ANY, DESTINATION CHARGES, AND OPTIONAL EXTRA.

Eric Peters Collection

Was it simply an unfortunate coincidence that AMC named this car after a mythical Scots—Irish beast known in Gaelic as the grumaimin, a "small, ill-humored gnome held to be responsible for the malfunctioning of equipment?" Either no one at AMC bothered to look it up or it was their way of forewarning potential buyers on the QT.

Good old Richard Teague, AMC's different-drummer chief designer in the early 1970s, is said to have penned the basic shape of what became the Gremlin (after about six rum and cokes?) on a Northwest Orient Airlines air sickness bag. This was a harbinger of the final product which was unveiled to the assembled automotive press on—yes—April Fool's Day, 1970.

The Gremlin was the first in a series of attempts by AMC to rebuild and expand its aging, obsolescent product line to compete with Ford, GM, and Chrysler. The trouble was that AMC had only a few loose coins jangling in its pockets by this time, hardly sufficient for the major product overhauls and modernization necessary to go toe-to-toe with Detroit's Big Three, let alone the rising tide of high-quality low-cost imports from Japan. To keep costs low, Teague pirated body and chassis pieces from the already aesthetically challenged Hornet and chopped off the back, creating the distinctive "what happened to the rest of your car, buddy?" look that became the Gremlin's signature design feature. Other points of interest included no disc brakes—not even optionally—no modern radial tires, and vacuum-operated windshield wipers on the initial 1970 model that hearkened back to the technologically sophisticated days of 1935.

Another classy feature that only AMC could have thought of was the exposed gas cap that jutted out on the flank of the car, very much like what you'd find on the top of a 50-gallon drum of sludge. It was frequently stolen, after which many owners would simply stuff an old, greasy rag into the hole and motor on. In 1977 the gas cap was finally relocated behind the rear license plate, which cleaned up the aesthetics somewhat. The downside was it now became a bit more difficult to Molotov cocktail the thing for the insurance payout.

Perhaps the oddest of these strange-looking cars were the 1977 and 1978 models that were fitted with a 2-liter four-cylinder engine supplied under the table by Audi. It was far too small for the 3,100-pound Gremlin. While Gremlins were squat and bizarre looking, up to this point they always had at least a standard six-cylinder engine, giving AMC a strong selling point over competitors—which generally had nothing more threatening than four-bangers under their skins. But with the Audi-sourced four-cylinder engine under its hood, the Gremlin lost even that small advantage: semi-decent acceleration.

As for one-time partner Audi, the now-upscale German automaker tends not to mention its disco-era relationship with AMC—much as Ned Beatty prefers to focus on his work in *Superman,* instead of his role as Bobby in *Deliverance.*

The "Kammback" Gremlin was initially offered as a budget-oriented two-seater and, in subsequent years, as a more luxurious four-seat coupe with a flip-up rear window hatch. The car shared many of its basic parts with AMC's other compact—the Hornet—including its ancient but reliable straight-six engines that dated back to the Eisenhower era.

The base price of the 1970 Gremlin was $1,879—$1,959 for the four-seat model—making it one of the least expensive new cars of its time. The stripped-down two-seater version was short-lived, however; after 1971, all Gremlins would be built as four-seaters only. Just 3,017 Gremlin two-seaters were built out of a total production of 671,475 units, making them collectible as Gremlins go.

In 1971, The Gremlin X appeared—and it wasn't just for Muslims. It could be ordered with either the standard 135-horsepower "3.8-litre" straight six, or the optional 150-horsepower "4.2-litre" version of the same basic in-line six cylinder engine. In 1972, V-8 power appeared in the form of the 304-ci "5-litre" engine, rated at a middle-warm 150 horsepower. But it was among the most powerful economy-oriented cars of the period. And you did get that humungous "X" decal for the extra shekels.

Like the Pacer, Gremlins could be ordered with flashy add-on stripes and decals (including a "Hockey Stick" side panel decal) and "Genuine Levi Jeans" seat covers. These also had the "genuine" copper rivets that could sear the owner's flesh if he was thoughtless enough to slide behind the wheel on a hot summer day while wearing shorts. (Making both these vehicles literal pains in the ass.)

Though Gremlin production ceased after the 1978 model year, the basic chassis was recycled by AMC and became the basis for the all-wheel-drive-equipped AMC Spirit and Eagle—the last cars AMC would build before the company's miasma of red ink finally caught up with it and the lights were turned out for good.

DATSUN B210
1974–1978

Long before Nissan changed names and became a brand name associated with desirable vehicles, there was Datsun and models like the snaggle-toothed B210. Today this car can be spotted on episodes of *COPS,* usually featuring a derelict being pulled from its back seat clutching a spray can of gold-fleck paint and a plastic baggie from which he's been inhaling his daily "huff." Otherwise, you can frequently see it modeling a trunk-mounted 3-foot-high pop-riveted airfoil in a dimly lit 7-11 parking lot as its owner filches around for loose change in the ashtray to cover the cost of a pack of Camels and a lottery ticket.

But it was with an onslaught of such stolid but sturdy machines as the B210 that Japanese automakers such as Datsun established their beachhead on American shores, pushing the Big Three back toward Detroit as effectively as Admiral Bull Halsey's serial kick-ass of the Imperial Navy 30 years earlier. Between 1973 and 1976 alone, Datsun's exports had burgeoned by an astounding 70 percent, and the company was well on its way to becoming the world's number one exporter of cars and trucks.

The homey little 1.2-liter 60-horsepower B210 may have not looked like much then—and even less now—but it was reasonably well-built and dependable, qualities most of the American cars of the mid-1970s consistently lacked. In a sea of ugly, under-performing cars, at least the Datsun would start most of the time. As a contemporary reviewer put it: "She ain't pretty, but she's as reliable as the sunset." The B210's only real weak points—as with other Japanese cars of the era—were grocery cart acceleration and a tendency to rust rapidly, a problem traceable to inadequate corrosion protection made worse by exposure to salt-laden sea air during trans-oceanic shipping. But people didn't buy the car for its speed, and the B210 could be counted on to run interminably, the drivetrain often outlasting the sheet metal. People snapped them up faster than pecan logs and meat snacks at an all-night truck stop. The rest is history.

The 1974 B210 could be ordered with a five-speed manual transmission and a tachometer, both relatively rare features in the 1970s, especially on economy cars.

A "Honey Bee" appearance package was offered that included a special yellow paint job and smiling bee decals. The GL got you chrome trim around the fenders.

The B210 was available in three body styles: coupe, sedan, and wagon. All B210s were rear-wheel drive.

The initial B210 series was retired in 1978; in 1979 it was replaced by the altogether different but familiar-sounding 210—no "B"—ancestor of the Sentra, which appeared in 1983 and remains in production today.

In 1982, Datsun became Nissan, but in the Japanese home market, "Datsun" lives on as the brand name for Nissan's pick-up trucks.

Jeff Glenn

RENAULT
Le Car
1972–1985

This car is rolling proof of the adage: "Nothing bad will happen to the person who owns a French car . . . because it already has."

The Le Car—also known as the Renault 5 in Europe—was a sad little runt of a machine with over-small tires and a rear end that begged to be kicked, just like the class loser back in junior high. Although it was conceived as a car that would "one-up" other small cars of the period such as the British Mini Cooper and even the Fiat 127, the Le Car as produced could have attended the same low-self-esteem support group as the Yugo.

It was launched in 1972 with the slogan, "Hello, I'm the Renault 5, in town and on the road . . . They also call me Supercar"—an audacious claim given the micro-displacement 850-cc, 36-horsepower engine that powered the original. It had roughly half the horsepower of a Chevette or Pinto.

Introducing Le Car

You'd need plenty of time to get your croissants in this one.

Later models were supplied with a noxious 1.6-liter diesel that smelled worse than the car looked. A later high-performance turbo model complete with bulging pontoon fenders at least made up for the ridiculous appearance by making tracks when you floored it. This version was actually quite successful on the track.

The Le Car sold through 1985 in the United States—1995 in Europe—and actually sold fairly well. Some three million were built, all told. Luckily, only a few remain roadworthy—and they're easy enough to catch and smash, if you come across a survivor.

As for parent company Renault, the French automaker formally abandoned the U.S. market in 1987 after selling the carcass of former partner in crime American Motors Corp. to Chrysler for $2 billion. However, Renault still has a bunion-covered toe in the North American market. Though few outside the car industry know it, Renault is partnered with highly successful Japanese automaker Nissan and may one day attempt to sneak some of its own cars back into the U.S. under the Nissan nameplate.

Sacre bleu!

- The Le Car had its name emblazoned in huge graphics along the side. (As if owners needed more help calling attention to their plight.)

- Despite its low power and weird, umbrella-shaped shifter, the Renault 5 won praise and accolades in Europe—including "Car of the Year," an honor bestowed by the BBC. Weird things happen where gas costs $4 a gallon.

- The company's U.S. slogan was "Renault: The One to Watch." It was far more important to watch the progression of rust through the Le Car's outboard torsion bar mounts, which had a tendency to disintegrate and impart interesting handling characteristics, especially during emergency accident-avoidance maneuvers.

- The Le Car was the last front-drive economy car designed with a front-to-rear (longitudinal) engine that pushed into the passenger compartment—rather than the side-to-side (transverse) mounting used by other manufacturers to maximize interior space.

- Historical footnote: Company founder Louis Renault was jailed for "trading with the enemy" after Paris was liberated by the Allies in 1944. He died a month later.

Lee Iacocca gets blame (or credit) for the Dodge Aries and Plymouth Reliant K-cars, but unlike the minivan, this one's really not his fault. He simply took the Turducken and ran with it.

Though Iacocca touted the virtue of K-cars aggressively once onboard as Chrysler's newly installed chairman (after having been fired by Henry Ford II), the K-car had been in development since the late 1970s—when it finally dawned on Mopar management that battling the surge of high-quality Japanese imports with vinyl-roofed Volarés and Cordobas decked out in "rich, Corinthian" leather probably wasn't going to turn out well.

Still, the change in scenery that took place between 1971 and 1981—the year of the K-car's launch—was dramatic. It had only been ten years since the Chrysler Pentastar ruled the streets with 375-horsepower 440 Super Commando Road Runners and 425-horsepower 426-ci "Street Hemi" V-8 powered Chargers, GTXs, and 'Cudas—cars with the vein-popping stage presence of Arnold Schwarzenegger at his Mr. Universe prime. But by the early 1980s, a "Hemi" badge on the fender of an Aries-K or Reliant meant a Mitsubishi-sourced "Silent Shaft" 2.6-liter four cylinder with a two-barrel carburetor—and 92 horsepower. No pistol grip shifter for you, buddy boy. Just dog dish hubcaps and an 85-mile-per-hour "federal" speedometer.

Chrysler's own engine—the 84-horsepower 2.2-liter "Trans-Four"—was the K-car's standard engine. It would entertain its owners with an erratic, surging idle caused by the problem-prone computerized spark-control unit that resulted in the engine's timing jumping by 2 to 5 degrees for no apparent reason. When Chrysler switched to a slightly less crude throttle body fuel injection (TBI) system in the mid-1980s, it created another form of in-car amusement. As one contemporary reviewer wrote: "Chrysler's TBI motors had a rather steep throttle tip-in, meaning if you tapped the rather stiff gas pedal, you got a lot of revs. Starting an automatic K-Car without jerking your passenger's neck required a bit of practice; with the five-speed's clunky shifter and abrupt clutch, driving smoothly was nearly an art form."

Yet this was the car that led to Chrysler's return from the abyss and enabled the company to go on to bigger and better things—like the minivan.

In Mexico, the K-car was sold as the Dart rather than the Aries-K or Reliant. Chrysler might have been worried about the problem Chevy had when it exported the Nova to Latin America. In Spanish-speaking countries, "Nova" can be translated as "doesn't go."

The K-cars, though pitiful and depressing, were a huge commercial success—and enabled Chrysler to return to profitability by 1983.

The 1981 models had bench seats for both front- and rear-seat passengers. The rear windows didn't roll down. (Some owners liked to pretend it was a very slow police car. "Settle down back there, ya skell!")

The price of a typical K-car was about $5,800 in 1981; this grew to $6,995 by the time the 1986 "Aries America" appeared—roughly 40 percent of the cost of a new Dodge Neon.

The 0-to-60 times varied from a low of 18.1 seconds to as sprightly as 10.6 seconds. Fuel injection and other improvements to the later cars accounted for much of the difference.

FORD PINTO
1971–1980

The Pinto was supposed to
have been a "worry-free" car, according to
the fundamental design philosophy enunciated by
then-Ford President Lee Iacocca, fresh off the success of
the Mustang and looking for another pelt to add to his belt. But
according to the class-action lawsuit later brought against Ford Motor
Co. over the Pinto's unfortunate tendency to erupt in a massive fireball
following an impact at speeds over 25 miles per hour, company engineers had
determined that it would cost about $11 per vehicle to reinforce the Pinto's
vulnerable and leak-prone fuel tank. That came to $137 million per year, versus a
much more manageable $49.5 million that Ford lawyers figured would have to be set
aside to pay off the families of the estimated 360 people who would be roasted to death
(or merely severely burned) in Pinto *auto-da-fes* each year.

Ford decided the lawyers' cost–benefit analysis was eminently sound business thinking
and did nothing to fix the Pinto, which gives you a good idea how much value was placed
on the lives of the proles who bought new Pintos. To make matters worse, it was later
determined that the actual cost of correcting the problem would have been only about *$1
per car per year*.

See how much corporate America cares?

Ford made an effort to attract younger buyers in 1976 by trimming out a Pinto in
silver and black paint and christening the resultant package the Pinto Stallion.
In addition to the special two-tone paint and black-out trim job, these cars
were fitted with the Mustang II's sporty bucket seats, full gauges (so
you could see exactly how slow you were going) and a
"competition" suspension system which may have been
intended to help drivers avoid rear-end collisions and
thus live long enough to pay off the loan.

Jon G. Robinson

4-Door Sedan

h, small economy car that's fun to dr

t with Squire Option

price, fuel and scheduled maintenance. It all
adds up to new evidence that Ford means value.

There's a 2-Door Sedan, 3-Door Runabout and
the Wagon that outsells them all, big or small.
A 2.3 liter 4-cylinder engine with solid state
ignition is standard. So are bucket seats,
rack and pinion steering and 4-speed floor shift.
Even a modest budget will cover options like
the new Stallion Group which gives your
Runabout special sporty exterior styling.

Pinto 3-Door Runabout with Squire Option (left)
features woodgrain vinyl paneling on bodyside and
lower back panel with bright surround moldings,
belt, drip and window moldings and wheel covers.
Easy-lift door opens to 29 cu. ft. of cargo space with
rear seat down. Shown in Tan (Code 6U).

Handsome Plaid Cloth Interior (right). Add touches
of luxury to your little economy Pinto with the
Luxury Decor Group: woodtone instrument
panel applique, deluxe door trim panels, custom
steering wheel, passenger door courtesy light
switch, rear seat ash tray, and more. Tan (Code DU).

For more details and illustrations, see your Ford Dealer
for a 1976 Pinto Catalog.

ard Features—Ma

edan—FUNCTIONA
gine* with solid state
shift transmission □
□ Front disc brakes □
ctAire Ventilation □ F
brake □ Flipper rear
□ Ford Lifeguard De

& COMFORT: Full
oth and vinyl bench s
ean-type armrest wit
oor-operated courtes
box □ Bright drip ra
s □ Hub caps.

e in California.
own are optional.

Notable Standard Features—Pinto
FUNCTIONAL: 2.3 liter 4-cyl. engine w
state ignition □ 4-speed manual trans. □ R
pinion steering □ Front disc brakes □ Di
Ventilation □ Inside hood release □ Bias
tires □ Ford Lifeguard Design Safety Fea
APPEARANCE & COMFORT: High-b
bucket seats □ Mini-console □ Bright win
moldings □ Carpet. **3-Door Runabout**—Ab
Rear liftgate □ Carpeted load area □ Fold
rear seat. **Wagon**—See Pinto or Wagon C

NOTE: Other items shown are optional.

71

The Pinto was offered as a two-door coupe; a three-door "Runabout" hatchback; and, beginning in 1973, a two-door wagon that was available with quick-to-peel fake wood-paneling exterior trim. Mercury sold the same basic car as the Bobcat. Both were equally flammable, however. (The three-door models had a new tagline: "Now with an extra escape route!")

Though most Pintos were factory-equipped with four-cylinder engines, a small 2.8-liter "Cologne" V-6 engine could be ordered at extra cost between 1975 and 1979; this engine was dropped for the final model year, 1980, when the only available engine was once again Ford's 2.3-liter four cylinder.

72

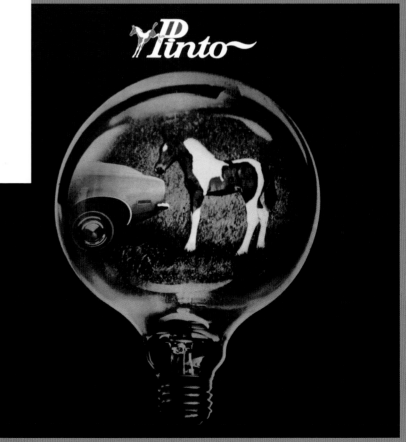

Peter Bodensteiner Collection

Adding a rear door and a seat that folds down to a Pinto that's already practical, makes it even more practical. For handy hauling. For

handy loading. That's the Pinto 3-Door Runabout. The easy handling, pneumatic-operated extra door gives you a cargo area of up to 41.3 cu. ft. With the rear seat folded down Runabout's carpeted flat floor is five feet long (from rear bumper to front seat back). Everything else is the same. Solid, sensible, durable, economical Pinto. Its responsive 1600-cc.

OHV engine gives you the same kind of economical mileage on regular gas as the little imports. And Pinto packs the performance to accelerate uphill and cruise long distances all day. The 4-speed transmission is

rock solid. Sports car rack-and-pinion steering puts authority in parking, cornering and turning. Pinto's ball joint suspension and wide, stable stance make remarkable road adhesion. Another

Pinto basic is that service intervals call for 4,000 miles between oil changes. Attractive alternatives in Pinto designability are the optional 2000-cc. engine which is bigger and beefier. Manual front disc brakes, SelectShift Cruise-O-Matic automatic transmission, SelectAire Conditioner, Luxury Decor Group, and others.

SPORTS ACCENT GROUP
Think dazzle! Then lay an optional Sports Accent Group on your Pinto. Available in White with Orange or Avocado lower bodyside.

Fold-Down Seat with carpeted load area.

paint 'tape treatment with matching vinyl roof, cut-pile carpeting, 'super-soft' vinyl trim, deluxe door trim panels, and an instrument panel with bright dress-up trim, parking brake and transmission bezel accents and deluxe steering wheel with woodtone insert. See the complete description on page 13.

STANDARD FEATURES:
3-Door Pinto Runabout. 4-cylinder 1600-cc. 1V OHV engine • full-sync, 4-speed manual transmission • high back, contoured all-vinyl front seats • reversible keys, 'keyless' locking • DirectAire Ventilation • 3-speed heater • Mini-console • fold-down rear seat • color-keyed carpeting in passenger compartment and load area • liftgate • 6.00 x 13 BSW tires • slotted

reminder system—positive reminder warning light and buzzer sounds when you shift into a moving gear, reminding front occupants to buckle up.

Sports Accent Group Interior with optional AM Radio. (Color BC.)

argent wheels and hub caps • Energy Absorbing Bumper System • front bumper guards • parking lamps • bright backlite, windshield moldings • plus all Ford Motor Company Lifeguard Design Safety Features including side door Steel Guard Rails and Uni-Lock shoulder 'lap belts with

Pinto 3-Door Runabout. Cargo-ready for hauling or cruising with Sports Accent Group (pages 9 and 13). (Color 9A with Orange.)

OPTIONS SHOWN
Luxury Decor Group (on left Pinto, described on pages 7 and 12), Sports Accent Group (above), White Sidewall Tires, Deluxe Bumper Group, Dual Racing Mirrors, Forged Aluminum Wheels, License Plate Frames shown are Dealer accessory.

For your convenience, each Pinto illustration is color coded, example (Color 3D.) Your Ford Dealer will be pleased to show you a color chip and actual swatches of vinyl roof and interior trim materials.

SPECIFICATIONS: 3-DOOR PINTO RUNABOUT			
Wheelbase	94.2"	Shoulder room	51.8"
Tread (front/rear)	55.0"	Hiproom	41.5"
Overall length	168.1"	*Front seat in rearmost position	
Overall width	69.4"		
Overall height	49.6"	Luggage: (cargo volume)	
Curb wt (at 1600-cc.)	2264 lb.	3-Door w rear seat folded	
		down, volume	41.3 cu. ft.
The Front Compartment:*			
Effective headroom	37.5"	The OHV Four (600-cc.)	
Legroom	41.2"	Carburetor	1V
Shoulder room	51.5"	Compression ratio	8.1 to 1
Hiproom	51.9"	Bore and stroke	3.19" x 3.06"
		Fuel capacity	
The Rear Compartment:*		and grade	approx. 11 gal., regular
Effective headroom	35.7"	Oil capacity	3.5 qt.
Legroom	31.5"	Transmission-4-speed manual floor shift	

Pinto 3-Door Runabout—practicality and style combined with Luxury Decor Group. (Color 5H.)

FORD PINTO 3-DOOR RUNABOUT

In 1973, a tuner named Ak Miller, working with Ford, created the "Pangra," a modified Pinto with a turbocharger and water injection capable of 15-second quarter-mile times; MSRP for this unusual Pinto was $4,605.

Another distinctive Pinto variant was the 1977 to 1980 Cruising Wagon, which nixed conventional rear window glass in favor of a single round porthole on each flank—set off with enormous three-color stripes and body-colored bumpers. It was a favored "love machine" of the time.

Major Pinto standard equipment included: "ventless" door windows, "slim-line" bucket seats, and a heater. (A fire extinguisher was a popular customer-added extra.)

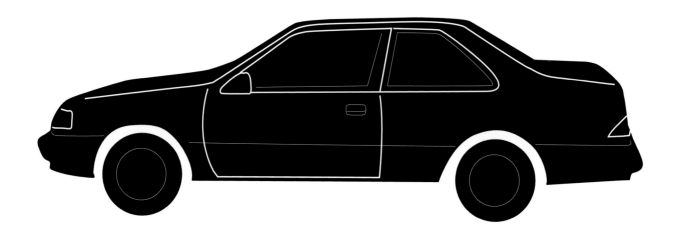

FORD TEMPO and MERCURY TOPAZ
1984–1994

Nobody much missed the boxy Ford Fairmont and its equally bland twin, the Mercury Zephyr, when they were finally recycled into more useful things like beer cans and zippers. But when their lumpy, buck-toothed replacements—the baleful Tempo and Topaz—appeared, it was clear to poor people everywhere that the future, contrary to the assurances of Elvis, did not look bright ahead.

Not merely ungainly and cheap, these cars were also feeble and embarrassing to be seen in. But wait, there's more! These cars were sent sputtering out onto America's highways and byways with numerous annoying and even dangerous defects—including ignition modules that caused the engine to quit at the least opportune times, such as the moment the driver stabbed the gas to cross a busy intersection, and faulty ignition switches that tended to short out and set the car ablaze. But that's not all! Also included was a defective wiring harness and alternator assembly—another fire-starter—that led to a recall of nearly 300,000 cars between 1988 and 1992—one of the largest single recalls ever.

Consumer Reports wrote that it had "received numerous complaints from consumers on fires, chronic stalling, unintended acceleration, paint peel and tie rod failure . . ." about the Tempo and Topaz. "Due to sub-par reliability," the editors continued, *"Consumer Reports* recommends that all 1989–1994 models be avoided," a rare blanket slam of an entire model, across several years of production. The accolades were not undeserved. "The 1984–1994 Tempo suffers from chronic stalling," *CR* stated, noting further that "In 1985, Ford tried to end stalling caused by faulty carburetors by switching to electronic fuel injection. Not only did stalling persist, but incidents of unintended acceleration were reported."

Ford—which apparently hadn't been cowed into shame by the still-fresh Pinto fiasco—denied the problems for years before reluctantly recalling an incredible 26 million vehicles, including just about every Topaz and Tempo ever built.

The automaker finally abandoned the problem-prone Tempo and Topaz in 1994, when these cars were replaced by the equally ill-fated Contour and Mystique—Ford's third or fourth attempt at building a "world car." (The Mystique quickly became known within the car industry as the Mercury Mistake.)

Both cars eventually died on the vine, but only after leaving a bad taste in the mouths of millions of Americans drivers—and making tow truck owners everywhere richer.

The Tempo and its corporate "twin," the Mercury Topaz, were among the first Ford economy cars to offer a modern front-wheel-drive layout—and were based on a stretched version of the subcompact Escort.

In 1986, an internal Ford document estimated at least 40 percent of the 4.3 million cars then under review would be returned as a result of problems with their ignition systems and stalling.

The Tempo and Topaz were powered by what Ford called a "High Swirl Combustion" 2.3-liter four-cylinder engine that developed 88 horsepower. (Many "high swirl" toilets are more potent.)

Two of the least-known Tempo variants are the Sport GL model that appeared in 1986 and the Electronic Part Time Four Wheel Drive model that became available in 1987.

For two years—1991 and 1992—Ford's 3-liter V-6 engine was available optionally. Very few were sold, though, and the larger engine, which had a tendency to blow head gaskets, was eventually deleted from the options list for the final two years of Tempo and Topaz production. (It could have been pitched as a safety feature: "Now with gaskets that blow before the car starts on fire!")

DODGE OMNI and PLYMOUTH HORIZON
1978–1990

IT BECAME A TENDENCY IN THE LATE 1970s to bestow optimistic-sounding names on increasingly scrunched-down and browbeaten cars that were at best proletarian-geared "transportation modules" about as enjoyable as day-old coffee and stale bagels. The theory was that people might be able to feel better about themselves with verbal shuck and jives—like replacing the title "stock boy" with "sales associate."

In the old days, when driving was something to be looked forward to, cars were usually named after vigorous animals or expansionist foreign policies. They were at least given names that suggested something positive, such as speed or graceful athleticism. Impala, Barracuda, Tempest, Monte Carlo. A man could proudly tell his buddies about his new Fairlane GTA or the Challenger 340 Six Pak in his garage. Even station wagons once had great names like Biscayne, Vista Cruiser, Estate Wagon, and Park Avenue Ultra.

But what, exactly, is an **"Omni"**? According to *Webster's* dictionary, it's more a prefix than a word in its own right: "A combining form meaning all, everywhere." As in "omniscient" or "omnipresent"? Perhaps Chrysler's advertising and marketing people figured that people might look upon the Omni as being the "all-car" that answered every transportation need. Except, of course, deriving any enjoyment whatever from the trip. This was a car to slug to your soul-sucking daily grind at the Shoe Outlet, mall food court, or after-hours gig as a minimum-wage security guard. All-miserable would have been much more accurate.

As for "Horizon," well, things were looking pretty dim if all you could afford was a cube-shaped little drone-mobile that marked you as a loser living on the periphery of the service-sector economy. Being seen in this car was a more effective route to maintaining a celibate lifestyle than gaining 400 pounds and going back to Mom and Dad's.

Weirdly enough, one of the fastest cars of the mid-1980s was a modified Omni—the Omni GLH and GLH-S. "GLH" stood for "Goes Like Hell," and it wasn't a lie. Carroll Shelby of Mustang GT350 and AC Cobra fame had a hand in putting the package together and even allowed the use of his name to help pitch the car. The GLH packed a turbocharged punch and as much as 175 horsepower in the GLH-S, which could cover the standing quarter-mile in less than 15 seconds. That was exceptionally quick for the time, right up there with V-8 Camaro Z28s and 5-liter Trans-Ams.

But even so, it was still just a powerful—and ugly—Omni.

The Omni/Horizon platform was also used to "spin-off" a pair of compact pick-up trucks in 1982—the Dodge Rampage and the Plymouth Scamp. One of the rarest sub-models is the Scamp GT, of which just 1,380 examples were built.

Byron Olsen Collection

Unlike the Chevy Chevette, Ford Pinto, and other economy cars of the era—which came as coupes, hatchbacks, sedans, and even wagons (in the Pinto's case)—the Omni and Horizon were never offered in multiple body styles, but were sold as boxy four-door sedans only. Po' folks don't need choices, right?

OMNI
IT DOES IT ALL

The initial run of Omnis and Horizons used a VW-designed 1.7-liter engine that developed 70 horsepower.
It was chucked in 1981 and replaced with Chrysler's own 2.2-liter engine—a version of which is still in use today in the Dodge Neon and PT Cruiser.

Special equipment that came with the Omni GLH and GLH-S models included a different camshaft; milled engine block (.020) to raise the compression ratio; long-runner intake manifold; slotted alloy wheels and 15-inch Goodyear speed-rated "Gatorback" tires; Koni shocks; and, on GLH-S models, a Garret/Air Research turbocharger that boosted output from 110 to between 146 and 175 horsepower in the "Turbo II" models. (These modifications helped you avoid being recognized as the owner of an Omni by driving faster.)

Omni lets you stretch out and relax.

Omni's concern for people of all sizes becomes quite evident when you take a look at the interior seating and stowage arrangements. In fact, a review of its wide range of seating options is your most obvious clue to Omni's travel-worthiness. Four doors open wide to welcome four adults into a choice of six distinctive seat designs.

The standard design is a handsome vinyl bucket seat with high back in blue, tan, red, and black, to complement your own favorite exterior color. An attractive option is a cloth-and-vinyl design in red or black.

If you order the optional Custom Interior Package, two choices can be made: an all-vinyl high-back style in blue, green, tan, or red; if you prefer, two-tone combinations of white seats with black, blue, green, tan, or red interior accents. The optional cloth-and-vinyl alternate in the comfortable Custom Interior is offered in blue, red, or green, and provides a very rich and luxurious appearance. Consult your Dealer about other items included in this package.

And if your tastes run to even more luxurious trims, there's an optional Premium Interior Package in two modes: all-vinyl with dual reclining seatbacks featuring an embossed vinyl; or as an option that features reclining seatbacks as well. Each seat comes with adjustable head restraints and is available in blue, tan, and red. You see, Omni designers made sure their comfortable interiors look as good as they feel.

A major ingredient in the Omni interior story, of course, is its luggage and cargo-carrying capability. The rear seat is a real two-seat accommodation, to start with, not just a simple padded bench. The "seat-up" luggage space provides 10.2 cubic feet (289 dm³) for local or long distance travel needs.

The standard security shelf panel conceals valuable luggage or equipment from the overly curious and cannot be moved until the liftgate is raised. The panel is hinged at the upper edge of the back seat and folds down to form the back-of-the-seat floor in the "seat-down" cargo mode.

Loading is aided by two gas-pressurized struts which hold the liftgate in place. Omni has a very obliging way of handling a lot of what cars are supposed to carry . . . from plants to tots.

The Omni and Horizon hold the distinction of being the first American subcompact economy cars with front wheel drive, which became the dominant layout for almost all passenger vehicles by 1990—living proof of the truth of Gresham's law about bad money (or ideas) pushing out the good.

79

Rochelle Schultz

AMC/RENAULT
ALLIANCE

1983–1988

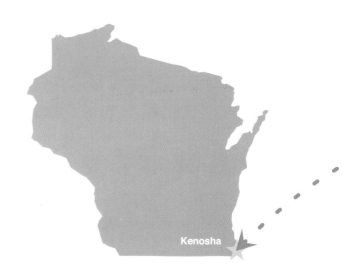

Kenosha

This 60-horsepower K-car wanna-be was sold from 1983 to 1988 in the United States under the desperate partnership formed by liver-spotted American Motors Corp. and French automaker Renault. An already terminal AMC finagled Renault into dishing out $350 million in early 1980s dollars to acquire a 46.4 percent stake in the company that brought the world such exemplars of style as the Pacer, Hornet, Gremlin, and Matador. $150 million went to modernize the AMC plant in Kenosha, Wisconsin, to manufacture the French-designed Alliance.

National Automotive History Collection

Not since Thomas Jefferson's Louisiana Purchase, whereby America got nearly half of the land west of the Mississippi River for pennies on the acre, had the French agreed to such an ill-conceived deal.

Even though AMC was at this point tottering on the verge of the abyss, with its life-support system on the same circuit as the air conditioning and the microwave, the French were sold on the idea of exploiting AMC's still-large dealer network to re-establish the Renault brand in the U.S. market. At first, things seemed to be going as planned; the Alliance was even named "Car of the Year" in 1983. A hatchback version called the Encore was released the following year.

Unfortunately for AMC and Renault, America was finally recovering its self-esteem after the Vietnam debacle and the misery of the 1970s. The "Gipper" had been elected president, and decent cars were gradually returning to dealerships. Renault's 50-miles-per-gallon wonder may have had appeal in Europe to a populace whose expectations had been stomped into the ground by $4-per-gallon gas, but Americans still felt they deserved more substantial cars. By 1987, AMC's death rattle could be heard echoing across Wisconsin as the just-modernized plant closed for good this time.

Renault gave up and went home, not even bothering to send flowers to the grave.

★ The Alliance was about 3 inches longer overall than comparable small cars of the era but still was among the lightest, weighing in at just under 2,000 pounds. It was also one of the most fuel-efficient, capable of up to 52 miles per gallon in highway driving, comparable to a modern gas–electric hybrid such as the Toyota Prius.

★ The Alliance featured what was called "three box" styling and could be ordered as a coupe, sedan, and eventually, a four-seat convertible.

★ A "Systems Sentry" idiot light package was offered that warned drivers of low fluid levels and the need to have the brakes serviced. This was high-tech stuff back in the early 1980s.

★ Though 1988 was the last year for the Alliance in the United States, the car continued to be manufactured and sold in Europe as the Renault R9.

★ A 1982 Car and Driver article described the Alliance's responses in a rapid lane change as making "one wonder if bowling balls are glued to the roof." (Actually, having a bowling ball on the roof might have added to sales.)

The last 2CV was built in July of 1990; all told, more than 5,114,966 of these cars were built over a 41-year period—making it one of the most widely produced and longest-lived models of all time.

Martijn van Well

While the original design specifications envisioned an air-cooled two-cylinder "boxer"-type engine similar in layout to the old VW Beetle's, the production model ended up with a water-cooled engine instead.

CITROËN 2CV

1937–1990

Imagine a moped without the cute factor or the power, and you've got a handle on the 2CV. This car started life in the mind of company founder Pierre Boulanger and his partner in crime Pierre Michelin—son of the tire dynasty founder. Boulanger wanted to create a vehicle that "would carry two peasants and 100 pounds of potatoes . . ." The result was the early prototype of the 2CV that would appear in volume only after the conclusion of World War II.

Unfortunately, it was not a casualty of that conflict.

The original pre-war 2CV—"Deux Chevaux," or "two horses"—featured a 9-horsepower air-cooled two-cylinder engine, comparable in output to a modern lawn tractor or small dirt bike. It may be the least powerful automotive power plant ever produced. There was also a canvas roof; no door locks or ignition key; and, just like a lawn mower, a pull-start system that made it easy for anyone to jump in and steal the thing for its value as scrap metal.

Still, the low-cost 2CV became ubiquitous in postwar Europe, where the unlucky losers of the Big One weren't in much of a position to motor around in two-ton chromed Detroit dreadnoughts with gigantic V-8s—and had to make do with this well-named "peasant's car."

The 2CV lingered like Limburger until the early 1990s—though thankfully not in the United States, where only a few were brought over—mostly to provide yet another way of making fun of the French.

In 1958, an interesting 4x4 version of the 2CV—the Sahara—was released. It featured separate front and rear engines, one to drive each set of wheels. Each engine could be operated independently and featured its own starter, choke, and fuel supply. (Unfortunately, at least one of the engines was always on strike.)

DAIHATSU CHARADE

1981–1987

Even its Japanese designers were unsure that what they had created was, in fact, a car—which perhaps explains the name. From its woefully inadequate three-cylinder engine to its crunched–Kleenex box styling, few cars exude penury and abject despair as completely and convincingly as the Charade.

This is a car that puts the "junk" in junkyard.

Daihatsu is actually a venerable brand—the oldest nameplate among the Japanese automakers. It was established at the beginning of the twentieth century and eventually became "Japan's biggest small car company," as it likes to style itself.

The Chiclet-sized Charade was introduced in 1978 and, though well-built, was so tiny, so feeble, and so expensive relative to other econo-boxes that it never caught on in the U.S. market. The company left by the late 1980s, leaving Charade owners out of luck when it came to service and spare parts.

While both the Charade and the mini-SUV Daihatsu Rocky have become curiosities in the United States, they are still significant profit-centers in Europe—where exorbitantly expensive gasoline enhances the appeal of ultra-small, ultra-efficient automobiles—and consumers apparently don't object to stuffing themselves like circus clowns into cars that are barely one step removed from Mattel Big Wheels.

Americans can thank their "hyperpower" stars that cheap and stable supplies of gas have spared them a similar fate.

National Automotive History Collection

 Daihatsu was the first Japanese car company to export to the United Kingdom and to Europe, where the company continues to maintain a strong presence. However, Daihatsu's foray into the U.S. market ended after less than ten years.

 The Charade was one of the first cars to apologize for itself with its own name. Later emulators of the concept include Mazda's Protégé (not quite a car, but working on it) and the Toyota Echo (a fading memory of better days).

Daihatsu Motors designed and built 275 electric cars for Expo 1970—nearly 30 years before electric cars would become available to consumers.

In 1983, a diesel Charade was brought to market that made the gas-powered version seem like an Indy car by comparison; but the thing did return almost 75 miles per gallon. (Compensation for the misery it inflicted on its owners, as well as those stuck behind it on the freeway.)

It's a little-known fact that Daihatsu is currently owned by Toyota, the second largest automaker in the world after General Motors.

Dishonorable Mentions

1975 Trabant

This mechanical offal—the product of East German socialism—was as exciting as a clam but not as sturdy. And it smelled far worse. Its two-stroke, two-cylinder 18-horsepower engine was notorious for producing a billowing contrail of smoke, while its unsynchronized manual transmission required at least a fifth of Stolichnaya to deal with effectively. The Trabant's ancestor, the F8 (and post-war F9) "Das Kleine Wunder" (The Small Wonder) had a body made entirely of low-grade recycled plastic, so the whole thing could be set on fire and reduced to a gloopy puddle of industrial effluent in a matter of minutes.

Jason Holt

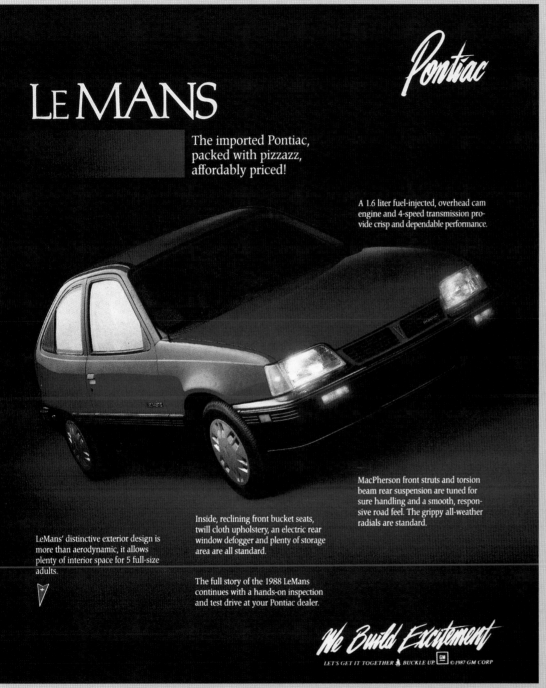

LE MANS

Pontiac

The imported Pontiac, packed with pizzazz, affordably priced!

A 1.6 liter fuel-injected, overhead cam engine and 4-speed transmission provide crisp and dependable performance.

LeMans' distinctive exterior design is more than aerodynamic, it allows plenty of interior space for 5 full-size adults.

Inside, reclining front bucket seats, twill cloth upholstery, an electric rear window defogger and plenty of storage area are all standard.

MacPherson front struts and torsion beam rear suspension are tuned for sure handling and a smooth, responsive road feel. The grippy all-weather radials are standard.

The full story of the 1988 LeMans continues with a hands-on inspection and test drive at your Pontiac dealer.

We Build Excitement

LET'S GET IT TOGETHER ★ BUCKLE UP. GM © 1987 GM CORP

Tom Heffron Collection

1989 "Pontiac" Le Mans

Not one of General Motors' better ideas, the "Pontiac" Le Mans of the late 1980s and early 1990s was actually a rebadged, Opel-designed and Korean-built Daewoo of notoriously poor quality (called the Nexia in its home market and the Vauxhall Astra in Europe). It came back for repairs under warranty (and afterward) more often than Elvis visited the refrigerator during his "husky" period—and was just as likely to fail in the middle of a performance. An "Aerocoupe VL" or "value leader" model was offered that came with no power steering, no air conditioning, and no power accessories.

1988 Ford Festiva

Introduced in 1988, this car didn't give its cash-strapped owners much to feel especially "festive" about. Were they supposed to be happy about being so hard up for money? The Festiva, like its awful contemporary the "Pontiac" Le Mans, was also Korean-sourced and shoddier than a politician's promise. Ford even removed power steering from the options list during the final few years of Festiva production, giving new meaning to the term "stripper." It was replaced after the 1993 model year by the Aspire—which hoped some day to become a real car, but never quite made it.

Jon G. Robinson

1990 Geo Metro

General Motors had done such damage to its reputation by the 1980s that it was deemed necessary to quit even trying to use an existing divisional brand name like Chevrolet to try and sell cars—especially small cars. Thus was born the supposedly "independent" Geo line and the slug-shaped Suzuki-built Metro. Offered as a coupe and sedan—with an "upscale" Lsi derivative optional—the Geo Metro (and the Geo name) lasted through the 1998 model year, after which GM once again felt safe enough to try selling its entry level cars exclusively under the Chevrolet banner.

Owner Jeff says, "At 40 miles-to-the-gallon, let 'em laugh!"

Jon G. Robinson

Samurai: The original fun meister, born to banish boredom.

Samurai Soft Top shown with accessory wheels and rear seat.

Unless you've been marooned in Antarctica, you probably already know the Samurai story. The original fun truck. The vehicle that's become practically the uniform of the day for an entire generation of young-at-heart drivers. It also has pasted more grins on faces than an army of standup comics. And why not?

This compact sport/utility vehicle, complemented by a miniscule pricetag, has boldly gone where no such vehicle has gone before—the fun zone. Attractively styled, and ruggedly built, the Samurai

Samurai Soft Top shown with accessory wheels, bumpers, western mirrors, winch, brushguards and off-road light package.

offers an irresistible combination of talent, looks and that certain something extra, a quality that goes beyond mechanical components and option packages — personality. The Samurai has it in abundance.

The lively and versatile Samurai is an ideal utility vehicle, an exceptional commuter, a fine off-roader and one of the lowest-priced sport/utility vehicles on the market. It's the answer to just about any transportation problem. For anyone who wants a fun and practical alternative to a second-hand beater, a small business who needs a rugged delivery truck or a family look-

ing for an addition to the family fleet, the Samurai is the perfect solution.

Available in Hardtop and Soft Top body styles, the Samurai is offered with a standard 1.3-liter engine, part-time four-wheel drive and a five-speed manual transmission. It features rugged body-on-frame construction, a two-speed transfer case and power-assisted brakes. The comfortable interior offers contoured, front bucket seats.

This talented little sport/utility vehicle is an ideal commuter vehicle, a rugged recreational vehicle, a great lightweight hauler and the best 4x4 bargain on the market. For the price, nothing else even comes close.

1987 Suzuki Samurai

This short wheelbase, micro-SUV was more prone to rolling over than an excited Labrador Retriever, a dangerous weakness magnified by the Samurai's snap-your-neck fabric-covered top. It was introduced in the United States and sold well through the 1989 model year, when Suzuki, under fire from safety advocates, replaced it with the Sidekick. This model looked similar but was four inches wider and several hundred pounds heavier—design changes intended to prevent purchasing the Samurai's successor from being a form of automotive seppuku.

Jon G. Robinson

1981 AMC Concord "Limited"

It wasn't the low volume of this Concord that truly earned the "Limited" designation, but rather its curtailed performance, weak styling, and all-around awfulness. It was particularly execrable when ordered with the optionally available half-vinyl landau roof, which gave it the appearance of a low-rung mob soldier with a bad toupee. "Relax," read the AMC ad copy for this reincarnated Hornet. "The luxury extras won't cost you extra." Maybe not in money; your self-esteem was another matter.

Jon G. Robinson

Professional VW mechanic Darryl says, "The thing to remember about a diesel Rabbit is that you have to adjust the valves every 20,000 miles, and it's about a $150 job. People weren't always willing to spend that kind of money on an economy car, and that's why you saw a lot of them smoking with soot all over the back end."

Jon G. Robinson

Jon G. Robinson

1977 VW Rabbit Diesel

Thanks to a poor initial design that resulted in stretched head bolts—resulting in a leaking head gasket at best or warped aluminum cylinder head at worst—the early VW diesel was a cheap car prone to very expensive problems. The 48-horsepower 1.6-liter engine's original design weakness was fixed after 1981, but while reliability improved greatly, even the later cars were unusually feeble—even by diesel standards—and often unable to maintain highway speeds on anything but absolutely flat roads. The built-in "smokescreen" provided by the stink-pot diesel engine at least served to alert other drivers to the 45-mile-per-hour obstacle up ahead they might otherwise have piled into. Like farm equipment and other self-propelled machinery, the VW Rabbit diesel should have been equipped with emergency flashers and restricted to the shoulder.

PART THREE

LOATHSOME LUXURY

Lee Klancher

BADGE-ENGINEERING AND RICH, CORINTHIAN LEATHER

A luxury car must offer much more than just transportation, just as a high-end restaurant better serve you something more than a microwaved Stouffer's lasagna.

But in the 1970s and 1980s, the luxury-car ideal faded like a $199 Maaco "presidential" paint job, replaced by fake wire wheel covers and vinyl roofs glued on renamed Chevy Cavaliers (the "Cadillac" Cimarron) and K-cars fitted with opera windows and "Maserati" crests (the Chrysler TC).

"Badge-engineering"—the auto industry's term for repackaging and re-selling an existing car under another brand name, or "badge"—has been around for a long time, but the practice got obvious and sloppy during the Automotive Dark Ages that lasted from about 1974 to 1990.

And if buyers didn't notice the quickie skin jobs, it was much harder to miss the slipshod engineering that plagued so many cars of this period, especially when you were stuck by the side of the road waiting for a tow truck or haggling with the dealer over yet another warranty claim. As bad as it was to pay double the cost of an ordinary car to get an ordinary car with ill-fitting wire wheel covers and "leather" trim only a step removed from extruded Naugahyde was the inability of these buckets, in more than a few cases, even to provide reliable transportation.

It was as though the state of engineering knowledge had regressed as a result of a collective knock on the head—or an infusion of some Chernobyl-like brain freeze. Not-ready-for-prime-time ideas were rushed into showrooms—such as the now-notorious "variable displacement" Cadillac V-8-6-4 engine. Even at the $50,000 level, expecting basic reliability—as in the case of Cadillac's beautiful but trouble-plagued Allante coupe—was often expecting too much. A high-end price was no longer a guarantee, or even a good bet, that you'd get a functional automobile.

Let alone "luxury."

It may be no coincidence that this ignominious era also saw the dawn of the "mass market luxury car," itself an oxymoronic concept when you stop to think about it. A luxury car is supposed to be uncommon—a cut above what the ordinary Joe can manage. If any bluto can buy one—or if there are five others just like it in the parking lot—then yours is nothing special. And by implication, neither are you. But all automakers must sell cars in order to make money, luxury nameplate or not. Cadillac, Mercedes, and other brands needed to reel in more buyers to stay in business, even if it meant diluting the gene pool and pandering to people who in better times couldn't afford a real luxury car.

So the Ritz became Motel 6, and, ever since, jangling a set of keys with a three-pointed star or Cadillac Crest doesn't quite mean what it used to.

Throttle body fuel injection (TBI) replaced the two-barrel carburetor in 1983; a new five-speed manual transmission with an overdrive gear was also offered, replacing the non-overdrive four speed used the previous year. A three-speed automatic was still optional.

Only 25,968 Cimarrons were sold during the first model year, far less than GM had hoped for.

The sticker price of the 1982 Cimarron was $12,181. This was almost twice the cost of the fundamentally identical Chevy Cavalier.

The 1982 J–car based Cimarron was one of Cadillac's first front-wheel-drive models, and the first compact-sized car to wear the Cadillac wreath and crest. (If by "wearing" you mean "attached just well enough to not come off in a car wash.")

The 1982 Cimarron was the first four-cylinder Cadillac offered for sale since 1914—and the first Cadillac to come with a manual transmission since 1953.

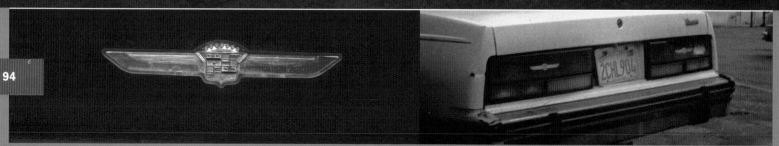

Jon G. Robinson

"CADILLAC" CIMARRON

1982–1988

In the 1920s and 1930s, Cadillac was a respected peer of Bugatti and Rolls-Royce, the "standard of the world" among luxury cars. By 1982, GM's premiere division had reduced itself to pawning off tarted-up Chevrolet Cavaliers, hoping no one would notice—at least until after the buyer's check cleared.

For thousands more than the cost of Chevy's compact economy car, Cadillac buyers were able to drive home in . . . a Chevy economy car with Cadillac trim glued to the fenders. In every meaningful respect the 1982 "Cadillac" Cimarron and 1982 Chevy Cavalier were identical. They shared the same GM "J-Body" chassis—and most major exterior body panels interchanged. Under the hood could be found the same 88-horsepower four-cylinder economy car engine, right down to its Adam's Apple two-barrel carburetor.

The final insult? For the first time in almost 30 years, buyers had to pay extra to get an automatic transmission. This was marketed as "sporty," when it fact it was just plain cheap: It cost GM less to use the Cavalier's manual transmission than to make the more costly automatic standard.

Even Cadillac blushed—initially describing the car as the "Cimarron by Cadillac" rather than a full-fledged Caddy, which of course it wasn't. Nine "hand-buffed" colors couldn't begin to paint over the ugly reality that GM's premiere luxury division was re-selling Chevys—cheap ones—at Cadillac prices. The "standard of the world" had become a K-mart Blue Light Special in every respect but the price.

Fifty years of building up the Cadillac brand-name to a position of unassailable integrity got flushed down the pipe by this single egregious bait-and-switch. Blinded by greed and short-sightedness, GM had hoped to rake in money by saving the time and development costs of designing and building a separate small car for Cadillac to sell, the way it had always been done in the past. Instead, sales slipped along with the brand's prestige as word got out about the Cimarron's guttersnipe origins.

To this day—more than 20 years after the Cimarron debacle—many people refuse to even consider a Cadillac as a result of the bad memories.

Cadillac let the Cimarron linger for six full model years, when it would have been far smarter to quietly sweep things under the rug and let time heal the wounds. Eventually, it might even have been possible to deny the whole thing ever happened—sort of like Henry Ford's authorship of *The International Jew.*

MERCEDES-BENZ 190
1983–1993

In the "coach built" era of the 1920s and 1930s, luxury cars were custom-ordered models assembled by highly skilled craftsmen—destined for an ultra-exclusive clientele for whom cost was no object. Only a select few could hope to own a Bugatti, Deusenburg, or Cord.

But by the 1970s, mass manufacturing and mass marketing had become an economic necessity for even luxury brands like Mercedes-Benz. Building no-compromise cars for the top 5 percent would have to take a back seat to selling cars, period—as many of them as possible, to anyone who could come up with a down payment. Thus was born the lamentable 190-Series—a Mercedes for people who couldn't afford a real Mercedes.

The "Baby Benz" continues to evoke snorts of contempt from appalled cognoscenti of the three-pointed star. Drive one to your local "EuroCars" dealerships for service and you'll know how the guy who owns a 1978 Mustang King Cobra feels at classic Mustang meets.

The four-cylinder-powered 190 didn't offer much to recommend it as a premium car. It was small—and with only 90 horsepower at first, it was hardly stronger than other economy compacts of its day. When Mercedes upgraded the cars to fuel injection—denoted by the "E" for Einspritz in the model designation—things improved somewhat. But even then, 122 horsepower was about what GM's small V-6s were whelping out in the mid-1980s.

In its favor, at least the 190s were rear-wheel drive—one of the few areas of real difference between the 190 and other low-renters of the time. Later models got better in terms of their performance, and a few V-6 variants even tickled the 200-horsepower mark. But sub-par (for Mercedes) build quality, so-so engineering, and ticky-tacky interior bits remained constant problems throughout the car's 11-year product life. Worn camshafts, oil leaks, and premature rust were among the more significant mechanical complaints.

Mercedes seemed more than a little relieved when it was time to "put down" the 190, which was replaced by the much better C-Class models that remain in production to this day.

The 190 episode is hardly mentioned in the company's literature. Like that other unfortunate period between 1939 and 1945, the years of the 190's production are a time the German automaker prefers not to talk about.

Eric Peters Collection

The in-house Mercedes term for the 190 Series cars was W201. (This was code language for "Blue Light Special.")

A very low production, high-performance model with as much as 235 horsepower was briefly made during the 1990 model year. (Like the Dodge Omni GLH-S, it didn't get any better-looking no matter how fast it went.)

In addition to the gasoline versions, a diesel-powered variant of the 190 was also available; this model was identified by a "D" in the model designation. (Also short for "dog.")

Many of the 190's interior and exterior dimensions are very close to those of a Saturn SL. Both cars are about 177 inches long, have about 90 cubic feet of interior space, and 12 cubic feet of trunk space. They also have four-cylinder engines—and about the same "curb appeal" as an old UPS packing box.

Instead of real leather, many 190s came with what Mercedes called "MB Tex" seat covers—a vinyl material not quite up to the level of the "rich, Corinthian leather" used on some 1980s Chrysler products.

Drivers of this lemon probably didn't feel especially "imperious" accompanying the wrecker back to the dealership to have their just-bought, top-of-the-line Chrysler's entire fuel injection system, intake manifold, exhaust system, and gas tank—almost everything except the doors and seats—replaced under warranty. These were just a sampling of the many appalling problems afflicting the last of the rear-wheel-drive V-8 Imperials. Not even the pull of having a geezing Frank Sinatra as paid pitchman—"The Chairman of the Board tells 'The Chairman of the Board' why it's time for Imperial," read the ad copy—could sucker the public on this one.

Almost $20,000 (a huge sum in 1980) bought you . . . a custom-bodied Chrysler Cordoba. And the Cordoba was basically just a gussied-up Dodge Mirada. And the Mirada, in its turn, pirated its transverse torsion bar suspension and basic body structure from the flea-bitten and ancient Plymouth Volaré (whoa-oh!—as the commercial jingle went) and lowly Dodge Aspen. It was like paying $300 per night to stay at Motel 6.

Few people checked in.

The first year—1980—was pretty dreadful, even by the standards of the time. Just 6,241 Imperials found buyers. But 1981 (by which time word had gotten out) was much worse. Sales toppled like Saddam's statue to just 3,466 units, which was barely more than half the tally of the previous season. This became a bleak pattern, as 1982 saw another halving of sales to 1,746 units—a disastrous performance repeated and amplified in the final year, 1983, when a dismal trickle of 932 Imperials dribbled out of Chrysler dealerships.

The Imperial was one of the final gasps of the old Chrysler Corp. before K-car derivatives replaced once-luxuriant names such as Imperial with "Aries-K."

Even those who liked the car's lines had to concede its flaws. One dedicated owner, who has preserved his 1981 Imperial with just 8,900 miles on it, says his car runs fine . . . "unless you try to go over 25 miles per hour."

"Then it stalls."

Sort of like the company itself did right around the same time.

In attempt to generate an aura of exclusivity—or to avoid any unpleasant associations—the 1980–1983 Imperial was not marketed along with other Chrysler models. Instead, it was sold simply as the "Imperial." (Much in the same way that Gallo Wines sells its MD 20/20 line of "fortified" wines under a separate label.)

The sticker price of the 1983 Imperial was $18,688, a large discount over the $20,988 ransom Chrysler demanded in 1982. (Giving owners a $2,300 head start on repair bills.)

The Imperial offered just one optional extra: an electric sunroof. (If you wanted it to close, that was another matter; see your dealer for details.) A digital dashboard was standard—as was erratic performance. Buyers could select from one of several interior schemes, audio systems, and wheel covers at no extra charge (until the warranty expired).

Although "rich, Corinthian leather" was not an available Imperial interior feature, "rich, Kimberly Cloth velour" was.

The standard and only engine choice was a 5.2-liter 318-ci V-8 with throttle body fuel injection—which had to be recalled as a result of persistent drivability problems and was dealer-replaced at no charge to the owner with a "lean-burn" carburetor that didn't work much better.

CHRYSLER IMPERIAL
1980–1983

Daniel M. Wing

MERCURY ZEPHYR

1978-1983

HISTORICALLY, a Mercury was always "more than a Ford—but less than a Lincoln." Until, that is, the 1978 Zephyr appeared.

This car was at its best a slightly warmed-over Ford—a Fairmont, to be precise. And the Fairmont was about as plain as it was possible to get, the automotive equivalent of a spinster librarian. The latter-day Zephyr was about as exciting, too—from its NASA motor pool in-line six-cylinder engine, boxy styling, and plastic egg-crate grille to its "driver's ed–grade" plastic and vinyl interior.

Poor old Edsel Ford was spinning in his grave at high rpm when the Zephyr nameplate he developed with so much love thirty years earlier was affixed to this Fox-bodied staple of demolition derbies and shopping mall security guard details. The suggestion that this car could claim any spiritual link to the classic pre–World War II V-12 Zephyrs is like comparing J. Lo to Bette Davis—or Ben Affleck to Cary Grant.

Ford brought forth the Fairmont/Zephyr twins in 1978 to replace the aging Ford Maverick and its twin, the Mercury Comet. As before, both coupe

zeph•yr (zef'er):
n. Something that is airy,

National Automotive History Collection

insubstantial, or passing.

- The Zephyr (and Fairmont) were eventually replaced by the front-wheel-drive Ford Tempo and Mercury Topaz in 1984, cars that made the Zephyr seem pretty good in retrospect.

- In 1980, the 5-liter 302 V-8 was replaced by a tiny 4.2-liter 255 V-8. After 1982, Ford and Mercury dropped the sickly V-8 entirely from the lineup. The 4.2-liter V-8 was the smallest (and least well-known) OHV V-8 Ford ever built.

- The Zephyr Z-7 coupe was marketed as a separate model and remained so until the end in 1983.

- A four-speed manual transmission was offered in the sedan, but not with the V-8 engine.

- From 1978 to 1980, a "sport" version of the Zephyr sedan called the ES was available. It featured a blacked-out grille, spoke steering wheel, and rear stabilizer bar to "improve handling and road feel"—ideally, as you drove the thing off the road into a swamp.

and sedan body styles were available: Ford's version was called the Futura, and Mercury's sad-sack cousin, the Zephyr Z-7. (A wagon version was also available.)

Despite their plain-as-oatmeal appearance, the cars actually sold pretty well—just as bad food and manufactured boy band music do today. The Zephyr's "success" was more a consequence of the fact that after a decade of ever-more-awful cars, the American public had grown accustomed to such automotive dreck—in the same way an inmate learns to appreciate his daily ladle of gruel.

But like a persistent case of tuberculosis, the Zephyr just wouldn't go away. The "Fox" body architecture that bowed way back in 1978 was still in use as late as the 2004 model year—forming the basic mechanical underthings of the 1994 and up Mustang.

CADILLAC
SEVILLE
DIESEL
1978–1985

As the second energy crisis in a decade kidney-punched an inflation-addled nation, several automakers began to eye the diesel engine as a way to attract customers interested in high-mileage vehicles. The diesel alternative seemed especially appealing to luxury car brands such as Cadillac, whose mighty road dreadnoughts slurped fuel at increasingly unconscionable rates.

It was by no means a bad idea. Diesel engines were (and remain) in much wider use in Europe, where gas has always been more expensive and fuel economy more of a selling point. And of course, most heavy trucks in the United States burn diesel. The problem was General Motors didn't have any diesel engines available—or at least, none that were suited to passenger vehicle service. A GMC straight-eight diesel from a big semi would never fit into a DeVille. GM's answer? A hasty conversion job of an already-in-service gasoline engine, the Oldsmobile 5.7-liter 350 V-8.

Unfortunately for the many unlucky souls who ended up getting "that great GM feeling," the 22.5:1 compression ratio converted diesel (versus the gas engine's 8.0:1) overstressed head gaskets, head bolts, and other critical parts never designed to handle the much greater internal stresses of diesel combustion—which relies on pressure-induced ignition, rather than spark, to make power.

Major service work—including complete engine replacements under warranty—became almost as commonplace as oil changes.

- The 1978 Seville diesel was the first domestic-built diesel V-8 passenger vehicle and the last one GM ever built for the U.S. market. As of the 2004 model year, no U.S. automaker offers a diesel-powered passenger car.

- Though it had a terrible record for early failure, when it ran, the converted Olds diesel V-8 delivered fuel economy in the mid to high 20s—outstanding mileage for a 4,000-pound luxury sedan at that time.

- In 1980, the Seville was reconfigured to front-wheel drive, becoming one of the first Cadillac models (in addition to the Eldorado) to abandon traditional rear-wheel drive.

- In 1980, buyers could escape the diesel by selecting the "delete option" 6-liter gasoline V-8, for which they received a $266 credit applied to the cost of the car.

- When the diesel engine was finally retired in 1982, it was replaced by an engine that became equally legendary for being a problem-prone, poorly engineered mess—the "HT4100" 4.1-liter gas-burning V-8.

Robert Murchie Jonathan Redford

The new bustleback 1977 Seville, Cadillac's "international" sedan, was the first victim to be saddled with the now-infamous diesel engine. At first it was merely a $287 option and buyers—the fortunate ones—could still get a perfectly serviceable (if underpowered) gas-fueled V-8. But by the dread year 1980, the diesel engine became the Seville's standard power plant, even as word began to spread about the diesel's propensity for spitting out its bits and pieces all over the road like teeth after a prize fight.

Even when it worked, the experience of driving a diesel Seville was not quite Cadillac. At full steam, the diesel 5.7 liter delivered just 125 horsepower—not much to move a 4,000-pound car. And it complained bitterly each time the driver asked for a little acceleration, coughing and sputtering like a goose being hand-choked for its pâté de foi gras and leaving a haze of oily smoke in its wake. It idled like a high-mileage Kenworth and assaulted owners and occupants with industrial-grade stench. Seville diesel owners had to stand in puddles of greasy sludge and handle oil-fouled diesel pumps at every tank-up. It was a disgusting—and financially draining—experience that poisoned the well for diesel engines in the United States.

Even today, nearly 30 years after the fact, many American car buyers remain leery of modern, purpose-built diesel engines solely on account of the foul memories of the GM diesel fiasco.

CHRYSLER/MASERATI TC
1989–1991

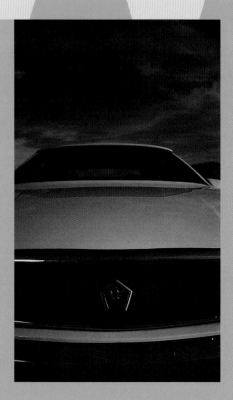

If you slipped a wino into a pair of Bruno Magli shoes, not many people would believe he was actually Pierce Brosnan out for an incognito stroll. Yet Chrysler Corp. thought that a similar quickie Italian makeover would work wonders for its K-car–based, front-wheel-drive Le Baron coupe. But instead of Bruno Maglis, the $13,830 (MSRP) 1989 Le Baron was fitted with an opera window, the Maserati trident symbol, and sold as the "Maserati TC" for $33,000—or more than twice the price of the Le Baron.

The TC was the result of Chrysler Corp.'s canny acquisition of a five percent stake in low-volume, low-profit—but high-prestige—Italian exotic car manufacturer Maserati, one of the auto industry's great names. Then–Chrysler Chairman Lee Iacocca figured he could boost the cachet of Chrysler's decent but far-from-exotic family of K-Car derivatives by canoodling the breed with the Italian thoroughbred. Maserati CEO Alessandro de Tomaso, as always in need of some stay-afloat cash, supplied the virgin offering of his company's name and reputation.

Thus was the hybrid "Chryslerati" born—an inbred, banjo-plucking, toothless mess.

Owner Chuck says, "The TC isn't badge engineering! It has an entirely different body structure, and the interior was all hand made in Italy . . . The TC's first engine was a four-banger, and it wasn't a hot car like the Allante. They got the V-6 later in the year, but it still wasn't the hot rod people wanted it to be."

Jon G. Robinson

♦ Chrysler seriously toyed with the idea of naming the TC the "Lido"—in honor of CEO Lee Iacocca. (Bet he's thankful that didn't happen.)

♦ Though the TC's 2.2-liter engine was mostly Chrysler-sourced, it did boast a Cosworth-developed DOHC cylinder head that resulted in a 200-horsepower rating. Unfortunately, automatic-equipped models were detuned to 160 horsepower.

♦ Chrysler had hoped to sell as many as 5,000 TCs annually, but the car did not sell as well as anticipated; just 7,301 were produced over the car's three-year run.

♦ "Pasubio leather" was a TC-exclusive feature. (Pasubio is an Italian tannery, not a mutant breed of "downer" cattle. Its claim to fame is being Peugeot's official supplier of seat leather.)

♦ The TC was the only front-drive, four-cylinder vehicle ever to wear the Maserati "Trident."

It lived for but three years, not fooling many on the way. Though not really a bad car as such, it was no more a Maserati than a Chevette is a 'Vette. First of all, the TC looked too obviously like the humble Le Baron it shared so much of its genetic makeup with—most glaringly its front-wheel-drive layout and 2.2-liter K-car–sourced power plant. Real Maseratis are all rear-wheel drive; none have ever had four-cylinder engines.

The TC looked like what it was, a custom job someone whipped up to make a Le Baron look a bit snazzier. But $33,000? That was like expecting people to pay $20 for a Quarter Pounder with cheese if it was called a Royale with cheese and served on a china plate instead of purveyed to you wrapped in greasy paper.

In 1991, the last year the TC was produced, a Mitsubishi-sourced 3-liter V-6 became available. It was more powerful and had two more cylinders, but it was nonetheless still far-removed from the heart that beat under the hood of the full-breed Maseratis of yore. Accordingly, the TC was mocked as a poseur almost from the get-go, and today is the only Maserati to have about the same collector car value as an old Renault.

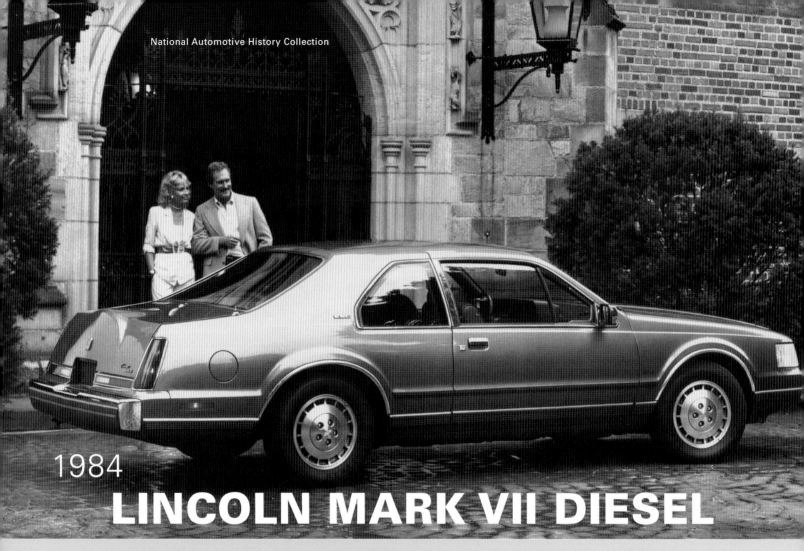

1984

LINCOLN MARK VII DIESEL

IN THE MID-1980s, one of the hottest luxury sport coupes around was Lincoln's Mark VII coupe. While GM was peddling flimsy front-wheel-drive Eldorados and pretty but problem-plagued Allantes, Lincoln actually hit one out of the park. The rear-drive Mark VII was a great-looking car that did credit to the capability of American stylists. It was hulky and fast-looking, with features and equipment that rivaled the world's finest cars. Even better, it could be fitted out in true "Hot Rod Lincoln" style by specifying the Luxury Sport Coupe (LSC) package. This centered around the same "high output" 5-liter V-8 used in the Mustang GT during those years. With as much as 220 horsepower on tap, tube headers, dual exhausts, and an aggressive sport-tuned suspension system, the Mark VII LSC was one of the most desirable luxo-sport coupes of the Reagan years and compared quite favorably to high-end imports like the Mercedes 450SL.

But there was a version of the Mark VII that didn't do as well as the rest. In 1984—the first year for the Mark VII—a 115-horsepower BMW/Steyr-sourced 2.4-liter straight-six diesel engine could be ordered in place of the gas-burning, 5-liter V-8. The diesel option was supposed to further enhance the "Euro" appeal of the then-new Mark. All it really did was remind people how wonderful it is that the U.S. government, unlike those of most European nations, doesn't place extortionate taxes on gasoline and thereby force Americans to drive smoke-spewing, death-rattling garbage scows—which is what the diesel-equipped Mark VII felt and sounded like. It could go farther on a full tank, but most people who experienced a ride wanted it to be over sooner rather than later.

The diesel Mark was bought by very few and did not last long; it was dropped with little notice or remorse from the product literature and options sheet, never to return.

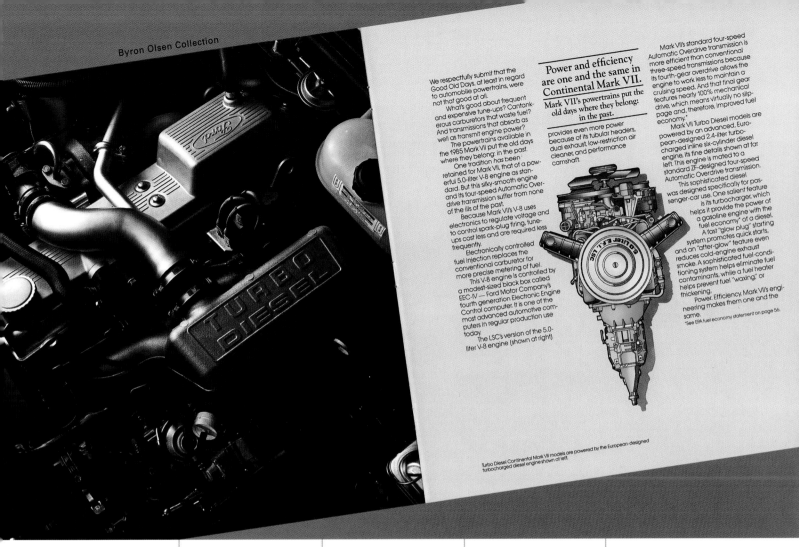

We respectfully submit that the Good Old Days, at least in regard to automobile powertrains, were not that good at all.

What's good about frequent and expensive tune-ups? Cantankerous carburetors that waste fuel? And transmissions that absorb as well as transmit engine power?

The powertrains available in the 1985 Mark VII put the old days where they belong: in the past.

One tradition has been retained for Mark VII, that of a powerful 5.0-liter V-8 engine as standard. But this silky-smooth engine and its four-speed Automatic Overdrive transmission suffer from none of the ills of the past.

Because Mark VII's V-8 uses electronics to regulate voltage and to control spark-plug firing, tune-ups cost less and are required less frequently.

Electronically controlled fuel injection replaces the conventional carburetor for more precise metering of fuel.

This V-8 engine is controlled by a modest-sized black box called EEC-IV — Ford Motor Company's fourth generation Electronic Engine Control computer. It is one of the most advanced automotive computers in regular production use today.

The LSC's version of the 5.0-liter V-8 engine (shown at right)

Power and efficiency are one and the same in Continental Mark VII.

Mark VII's powertrains put the old days where they belong: in the past.

provides even more power because of its tubular headers, dual exhaust, low-restriction air cleaner, and performance camshaft.

Mark VII's standard four-speed Automatic Overdrive transmission is more efficient than conventional three-speed transmissions because its fourth-gear overdrive allows the engine to work less to maintain a cruising speed. And that final gear features nearly 100% mechanical drive, which means virtually no slippage and, therefore, improved fuel economy.*

Mark VII Turbo Diesel models are powered by an advanced, European-designed 2.4-liter turbocharged inline six-cylinder diesel engine, its fine details shown at far left. This engine is mated to a standard ZF-designed four-speed Automatic Overdrive transmission.

This sophisticated diesel was designed specifically for passenger-car use. One salient feature is its turbocharger, which helps it provide the power of a gasoline engine with the fuel economy of a diesel.

A fast "glow plug" starting system promotes quick starts, and an "after-glow" feature even reduces cold-engine exhaust smoke. A sophisticated fuel-conditioning system helps eliminate fuel contaminants, while a fuel heater helps prevent fuel "waxing," or thickening.

Power. Efficiency. Mark VII's engineering makes them one and the same.

*See EPA fuel economy statement on page 56.

Turbo Diesel Continental Mark VII models are powered by the European-designed turbocharged diesel engine shown at left.

In addition to the LSC edition, Mark VIIs were also offered in glitzy Bill Blass and Gianni Versace designer editions.
Of the two, the more tasteful Bill Blass versions sold better.

The 1984 to 1992 Mark VII was built on a modified version of Ford's "Fox" platform—which is also used by the Ford Fairmont and Mustang.

In 1985, the LSC Mark VII became the first American production car to come from the factory equipped with four-channel anti-lock disc brakes as standard equipment.

The diesel engine option lasted just two years, from 1984 to 1985, after which it was dropped. (Owners of diesel Marks must register with the EPA to be eligible for Superfund clean-up dollars.)

To help crutch the 2.4-liter diesel and improve the car's acceleration, diesel-powered Mark VIIs were fitted with a more aggressive 3.73 rear axle (other Marks came with 3.08 rear gears).

STERLING
825 & 827
1987–1991

One of the more bizarre (and unrewarding) automotive partnerships in all of automotive history was the early-1980s collaboration between British Land Rover and Honda—a pairing destined to be as enduring as the Hitler–Stalin non-aggression pact, and just as awkward.

At the time, Land Rover was among the most established and well-regarded names in the car industry. It had old-world cachet, but equally old-world and out-of-date models—and not much money in the kitty to finance the development of new ones. Honda, meanwhile, was desperate to establish its then-new Acura luxury division at a time when the terms "Japanese" and "luxury car" were not often used together in the same sentence. While Acura would go on to great things, the half-breed spawn of this odd one-night stand would go down as one of the greatest commercial flops ever.

The Sterling 825 and 827 were more or less first-generation Acura Legends with different grilles and body panels, and they used the same basic Honda-sourced drivetrains as their Acura cousins. Given Acura's "sterling" reputation today as a manufacturer of first-class luxury cars—and the well-known success of the Legend in the United States—it's hard to understand why the essentially similar Sterling 825 and 827 went belly-up so quickly. Mostly, it was due to stupendously inept marketing and a weak dealer chain. Rover dealers in the United States, used to selling go-anywhere SUVs, never quite knew what to do with the cars. And the general public never quite figured out what a "Sterling" was—or had any motivation to find out.

Those who did buy one quickly encountered defeating problems such as dashboards that turned a hideous green in the sunlight and other fit, finish, and build quality issues related to the car's chintzy British-sourced exterior pieces, which, after the car's discontinuation, became all-but-impossible to find.

Like Strom Thurmond did, a Sterling will run almost forever thanks to its Honda/Acura engineering. But it will look a lot like old Strom did, too.

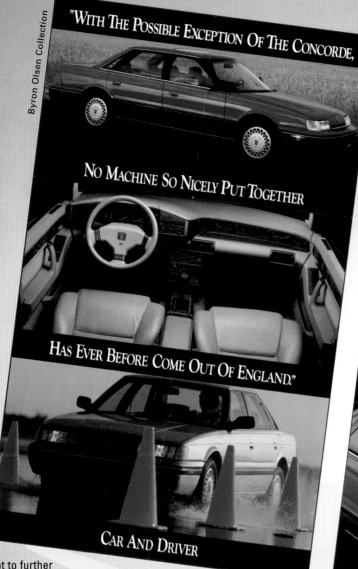

In attempt to further establish the car's English bona fides (and put some distance between Land Rover and Honda), Sterling offered an "Oxford Edition" of the 827 that was fitted with Jaguar-style interior appointments. Unfortunately for Sterling, people who wanted a Jag weren't interested in a Sterling trying to be a Jag.

Even though Sterling has been out of production for less than 15 years, hardly anyone outside the car industry is familiar with the name or can tell you even a few things about the cars themselves. (Negatives were burned, pictures airbrushed, and dealers and owners alike entered the witness protection program.)

The 2.7-liter V-6 engine in later model Sterling 827s is basically the same engine used in 1995 to 1997 V-6 Honda Accords, so any Honda or Acura dealer can service a Sterling.

Land Rover went back to selling SUVs exclusively in the United States after the failure of the Sterling.

In the European home market, the Sterling was sold as the Rover 800; hatchback and turbo-diesel versions were eventually offered.

WHEN IT APPEARED IN 1966, the front-wheel-drive Oldsmobile Toronado was a show-stopper—one of those "gotta-have" cars that young men pine for almost as much as cheerleaders. The undulating bodywork, hunkered over four fat tires, was wild-looking, almost like the liquid metal character in *Terminator 2.* And the "Rocket V-8" under the Toro's long hood lived up to its name, smoking the tires through the indestructible, chain-driven turbo-hydramatic transmission.

Twenty years later, a miserable pretender appeared, wearing the Toronado name but partaking of none of the old car's glory. About all the two machines had in common was front-wheel drive, which by the mid-1980s had become *the* defining characteristic of an economy car. Certainly not the legacy of the supercharged Cord 810 of the 1930s—which pioneered the FWD layout—or the elegant, V-8 Toronado of the late 1960s.

Sales shrank along with the downsized car, plummeting 62 percent from 1985, the last year for the decent-sized model, to 1986, the debut of the "all new" model. The Trofeo package, which was available until the Toronado's demise in 1992, was Oldsmobile's palsied attempt to buck up the latter-day Toro's almost complete lack of style. But no matter the gewgaws, it was still just a small car trying to look big. Even with every Atari-like electronic gadget GM could throw at buyers, only 15,040 of these diminished Toronados found homes during the first year, including Trofeos—one of the worst-ever showings for a new GM vehicle.

When production ceased after the 1992 run, a venerable name was mercifully shelved for good. Though it wasn't obvious at the time, Oldsmobile itself would be getting the Big Needle just ten years later, when GM announced the end of the line for America's oldest car brand due to declining sales and general lack of interest.

Classic car pricing guides list the retail value of an "excellent condition" 1987 to 1992 Trofeo at less than $3,000—*about one-third the cost of a still-drivable 1966 Toronado.*

OLDSMOBILE TORONADO TROFEO
1987–1992

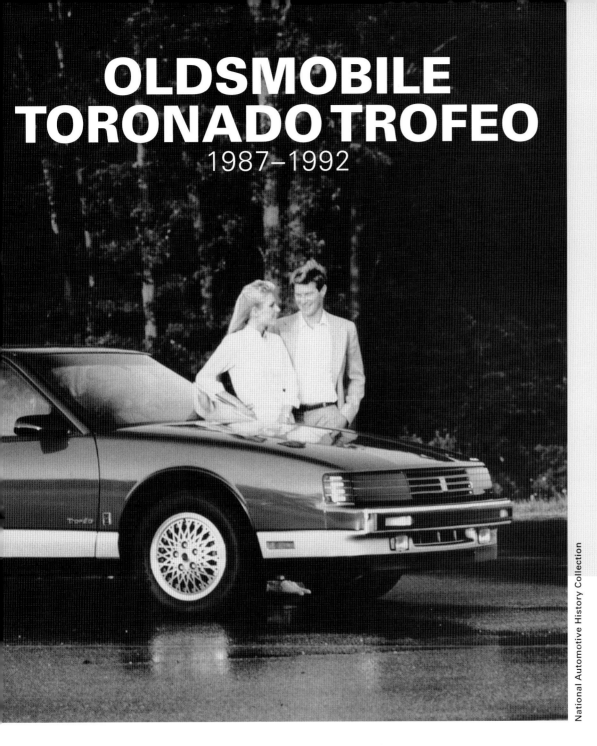

Among its claims to fame, the Trofeo was fitted out with an "FE3" sport suspension, hidden headlights, and an elaborate Visual Information Center (VIC) with a color video screen and the ability to display 52 separate readouts including a date book and calendar. (Every Trofeo came with an out-of-work actor from *Battlestar Galactica* or *V* to explain the use of the then-futuristic monitor.)

In 1990, Oldsmobile added about a foot to the Trofeo's overall length, but interior dimensions remained the same. 1990 was also the first year for a driver's side air bag—making it harder to "shed one's container" by slamming the thing into a concrete wall.

National Automotive History Collection

The Trofeo's V-6 engine produced 170 horsepower by the final year of production in 1992—about 100 less than the original 1966 Toronado's Rocket V-8.

Only about 1,000 Trofeo's were sold with the busy-looking Visual Information Center and the hands-free cellular phone option—making them among the rarest (if least valuable) latter-day Toronados.

CADILLAC
ALLANTE
1987–1993

The Allante, as Marlon Brando's character in *On the Waterfront* complained, "coulda been a contender." Designed to be an American exotic that would compete with ultra-luxury roadsters like the Mercedes SL, the Allante had an admittedly beautiful body penned by the Italian masters at Pininfarina studios, the same people who sculpt Ferrari and Maserati exteriors. But the problem with the Allante two-seater was never its looks. What turned this magic coach into a pumpkin was the car's dreadful initial quality, exorbitant price, and the less-than-world-class performance of its 170-horsepower 4.1-liter and (later) 200-horsepower 4.5-liter V-8s.

GM eventually sorted out the biggest flaws, most notably ditching the out-of-date (and underpowered) 4.1- and 4.5-liter OHV V-8s after 1992 in favor of the much more credible 4.6-liter DOHC Northstar V-8 that is still in use in new Cadillacs today. Unfortunately, the damage had been done by then, and there was no rehabilitating the Allante's reputation as an expensive lemon that was, as one reviewer put it, "riddled with body hardware problems," such as a leaky, poorly-fitted convertible top.

By 1993, the Allante's MSRP was approaching $70,000—well into the six figures in today's dollars—yet buyers could select the similar (and also Northstar-powered) Eldorado coupe—a much more solidly built machine that didn't need a 747 airlift from Turin or constant hand-holding—for almost $30,000 less. The Allante may have looked good, but it didn't look good enough to forgive its many flaws.

That final year saw just 4,670 Allantes out the door before the line closed down for good.

A "low cost" soft-top-only model without the all-weather hard top carried an MSRP of $51,500, about $7,000 less than the top-of-the-line version.

Specially modified 747 jetliners were used to transport partially finished Allante bodies from Italy to their final assembly point in Detroit, where the drivetrains, suspensions, and interiors were fitted before delivery to Cadillac dealers. The shipping costs involved were part of the reason for the finished car's exorbitant price.

Only a few of the later, Northstar-equipped models are worth much more than $15,000 today.

The first 1987 Allante had just 170 horsepower; the final Northstar-equipped 1993 model had 295. The Allante's descendant, the 2004 XLR, has a 320-horsepower version of the same Northstar V-8.

Northstar-equipped Allantes were quick cars, capable of reaching 60 miles per hour in less than six seconds. (This came in handy when trying to get back home and into the garage before it started raining.)

MASERATI BITURBO

1984–1994

THE ONLY ITALIAN MASTERPIECE YOU CAN DRIVE TO WORK.

If you're looking for something in marble, the average Italian masterpiece will run you six, seven million dollars. But if you'll take steel and sumptuous leather, may we suggest the Biturbo. Price, $27,000.

Twin turbos. Zero to sixty in 6.8 seconds. Handstitched leather seating. Handbuilt 2.5 liter V-6 that Car and Driver calls "a beautiful piece of metal sculpture." Maserati Biturbo. The second Italian Renaissance has begun.

THE ITALIAN TRADITION.

For a test drive at a Maserati dealership, call 301-646-3630. East. Or 415-775-3721. West.

"Fiat"—according to an old joke—may be short for "fix it again, Tony," but for the ultimate in distilled mechanical torture, few cars can rival this twin-turbocharged unfortunate from the skunk works of Alessandro de Tomaso.

The Biturbo coupe was one of those "affordable" luxury-exotics that turned out to be anything but. To quote the August 1990 issue of *Road & Track*:

"Mis-set carburetor float levels caused the engines to stumble during left turns, pick-up wires in the distributor cracked from the heat, water ran through cylinder sleeves, fluids leaked from faulty seals throughout the drivetrain, fuse boxes melted, and coolant temperature warning lights came on even when the engines weren't overheating. Clutches, timing-belt tensioners, and water pumps had to be redesigned early on."

And that's while the cars were still under warranty. Woe to the wretch who bought a used Biturbo.

Most of the problems with the car were the result of Maserati's low-volume operation and limited resources. Adequate time to sort the cars out properly just wasn't there, and the cars left the factory in what would be considered "pre-production state" by a larger automaker. Though the basic design of the Biturbo's 2-liter Merak-derived V-6 engine was sound, the rest of the car would viciously nickel-and-dime its owner to death with "little things" that would drive all but those truly devoted to its survival into the toolbox for a large ball peen hammer. Many an owner was probably sorely tempted to leave it abandoned and idling with the windows rolled down in a seedy neighborhood—and hope for a decent settlement from the insurance company.

While later cars were somewhat better in the reliability department, it wasn't enough to restore much-abused buyer confidence in the Maserati brand, which slinked away from the U.S. market after the 1991 model year. The company later went bankrupt, but was resuscitated once again, this time by Ferrari. 2004 saw the introduction of the first all-new Maserati model in more than ten years—the reborn Quattroporte.

There's no mention of the old Biturbo in the current product literature.

Power output of the Biturbo's V-6 ranged from 185 horsepower in 1984 to as much as 225 in 1989, when the engine was enlarged from 2 liters to 2.5 and Weber Marelli electronic fuel injection replaced the iffy two-barrel Weber carburetor used on earlier models.

Performance of the Biturbo was always respectable; even the first models could make it from 0 to 60 miles per hour in about 7 seconds. The later 225-horsepower versions were even faster—when they ran.

In 1985, a rare E model Biturbo was briefly offered that featured either dual air-to-air or air-to-liquid intercoolers that increased engine output to 205 horsepower; these cars could reach 60 miles per hour in about 6.3 seconds.

In 1986, a convertible Spyder version was offered; these were two-seaters only and had a shorter wheelbase than the coupe. The 1991 Spyders are considered among the most collectible of Biturbo models.

A 1984 Biturbo coupe cost about $26,000 when new, depending on options. Many owners found the purchase price worked out to a down payment on future service and upkeep costs.

POWER CORRUPTS. ABSOLUTE POWER CORRUPTS ABSOLUTELY.

In the Italian Renaissance the word for power was Machiavelli. In the second Italian Renaissance, the word is Maserati. Only Maserati would dare arm a V-6 passenger car engine with the same twin turbos found only on Formula One race cars. While lavishing the cockpit with racing instrumentation and handstitched leather appointments befitting a driver of neo-Medici aspirations. Result? The Maserati Spyder convertible, a mating of absolute power and absolute luxury. Under $32,000, plus state and local taxes. The second Italian Renaissance has begun.

THE ITALIAN TRADITION.

For a test drive at a Maserati dealership, call 301-616-3630, East. Or 415-775-3721, West.

National Automotive History Collection

115

National Automotive History Collection

1981 **CADILLAC V-8-6-4**

Like the ill-fated converted Oldsmobile V-8 diesel—whose grim memory plagues GM's reputation to this day—the one-year-only "modulated displacement" version of the 6-liter 368-ci Cadillac V-8 will surely go down in automotive history as one of the best ideas gone horribly wrong to ever reach production.

It all sounded great when the concept was first revealed: a large engine that could shut down some of its cylinders under light load (when they weren't needed to propel the car), but that could automatically (and smoothly) bring them back online whenever driving conditions demanded more power, such as when passing. The "modulated displacement" system was touted as being the best of all possible worlds in one package—the economy of a four-cylinder with the performance of a traditional V-8.

But the state of microprocessor development in 1981—when Ataris and *Pong* were considered "high-tech"—was not quite up to the job, and the crude mechanicals only exacerbated the difficulties of making the V-8-6-4 work as its designers had envisioned. It wasn't smooth—the engine would lurch or make noises most people only hear coming out of a slaughterhouse—and it wasn't reliable or especially efficient, either. To move a full-size boat like the Fleetwood with just 140 horsepower is no easy thing.

Though imaginative, the V-8-6-4 couldn't live up to the promises made by General Motors. It was exactly the last thing a by-now-reeling Cadillac needed on top of the still-festering diesel imbroglio. (The J-Car/Cavalier/Cimarron mess was yet to come.)

116

It would take more than 20 years for Cadillac to make significant inroads toward rehabilitating its image; more people remember the disasters of the late 1970s and early 1980s like the V-8-6-4 than the brilliance of pre- and post-war Cadillacs—when the marque was able to call itself "standard of the world" without anyone losing control of their bladder.

- Cadillac hyped the V-8-6-4 as "Answering Today's Needs With Tomorrow's Technology." (In actual use, tomorrow's technology was more like yesterday's technology built with last weekend's parts, when what was really needed was the day after tomorrow's technology, or perhaps even a week from next Tuesday's.)

- The V-8-6-4 was offered for just one model year, 1981. It could be ordered in Eldorado, Fleetwood, and DeVille models. The equally problem-plagued HT4100 V-8 replaced the V-8-6-4 in 1982.

- Another one-year-only feature used with the V-8-6-4 was an "MPG Sentinel" that displayed which cylinders were in operation, as well as readouts of instantaneous miles-per-gallon. (Someone at GM had found a use for the leftover soundboard and blinking LEDs pirated from the remains of Twiki—the mechanical Mini-Me from *Buck Rogers in the 25th Century*.)

- The V-8-6-4 engine used a solenoid-activated blocker plate to shift the pivot point of rocker arms that would otherwise open and close intake and exhaust valves, thus effectively "shutting down" unneeded cylinders, which helped to save fuel. A microprocessor governed the system's operation. Pulling off a few plug wires would have accomplished the same thing for a lot less money.

- In 2003, General Motors announced it will offer an updated "displacement on demand" system similar in concept but with modern electronic controls, perhaps as soon as 2004 or 2005. (Which really would be next year's technology for something thought of over twenty years ago for today's driver with tomorrow's car . . . no, wait, yesterday's driver in next Arbor Day's car that . . . oh, never mind.)

117

ZiL LIMOUSINE

The Soviet Union's best copy of a 1975 AMC Matador served leaders ranging from the living-embalmed Leonid Brezhnev to rummy Boris Yeltsin, who in one of his few sober moments dumped his state-provided ZiL in favor of a "decadent" Western Mercedes. Current Russian President Vladimir Putin reportedly has two ZiLs in his fleet, but his government has dramatically cut back on orders for new ones. The Zavod Imeni Lihacheva (hence "ZiL") factory, however, still annually churns out about a dozen of these austere and funereal chariots of the class struggle.

The ZiL nameplate dates back to the 1930s and 1940s, when it was merely a copy (literally) of the hulking Packard 180. Stalin's henchmen wrapped one up and sent it back to the Motherland for study. In a couple of months, the ZiL appeared, much to the delight of Uncle Joe.

It would be years, however, before Soviet stylists learned to emulate the infinitely greater design genius of American Motors Corp. and pushed the car to nearly 20 feet and 3.5 tons of torpid, top-heavy, taxi-cab-meets-hearse awfulness.

The ZiL was about as luxurious and innovative as things got in the old Soviet Union—probably part of the reason why today there is no Soviet Union.

The **heaviest** known car on record is the ZiL 41407 stretch limo built for ex-Soviet leader Mikhail Gorbachev; it weighed nearly six tons—and was almost as big as Gorby's port wine stain.

Late-model ZiLs are powered by a monster 7.7-liter V-8 that develops in excess of 300 horsepower. Both five- and seven-passenger versions of the ZiL were made.

Though carburetors have been dead in the West for nearly 20 years, new ZiLs still used them (as of 2003) instead of more up-to-date fuel injection. Apparently, only the proletariat need concern itself with emissions or fuel economy; ZiLs average about six miles per gallon—about half what a new Bentley Arnage R can deliver.

The most costly ZiL is model number 41052, equipped with bullet-proof glass and armor plating reportedly designed to withstand a grenade thrown by an angry Chechen rebel. The car cost more than $500,000 to construct and was among the last cars commissioned by former Soviet leader Leonid Brezhnev. ($10,000 dollars went to the onboard containment system that protected his massive eyebrows from nuclear attack.)

Both rear- and front-wheel-drive versions of the ZiL were produced.

Actually a 1965 ZiL 111-G limousine. Please don't throw us in the Gulag.

119

Dr. Leslie Sheldon

1974 AMC AMBASSADOR

Name a car "Ambassador," and it better have something to offer in the way of style and good taste. Unfortunately for long-dead American Motors Corp., the mid-1970s Ambassador sedan made about the same impression on the American buying public as Nazi Foreign Minister Joachim Von Ribbentrop did on the Queen of England when he paid a visit to the Court of St. James and gave her a stiff-armed sig heil.

Designed and marketed to compete with GM, Ford, and Chrysler's large luxury cars, the oddly-styled Ambassador found few admirers. Instead of building up AMC, it only sponged desperately needed operating capital away from the research and development of new models that might have kept America's struggling fourth automaker on the respirator a little longer.

Not content with having produced such winners as the Matador, Gremlin, and Hornet, AMC stylists did their best to create what may go down as America's strangest-looking modern sedan.

A jutting front end with weirdly disproportionate lines suggested a mechanical incarnation of a freakish, steroid-addled pro-wrestler. The headlights bulged out like a gut-hooked river catfish. Overall, it looked more Eastern European than American—and it's worth observing that latter-day Soviet ZiL limousines seem to be blood kin.

Some body panels are probably even interchangeable.

The Ambassador paid its last state visit to AMC dealer showrooms in 1974, leaving the Matador to do the honors thereafter. Thirteen years later, the last dying embers of AMC would flicker, then go out forever following the short-lived partnership with French automaker Renault.

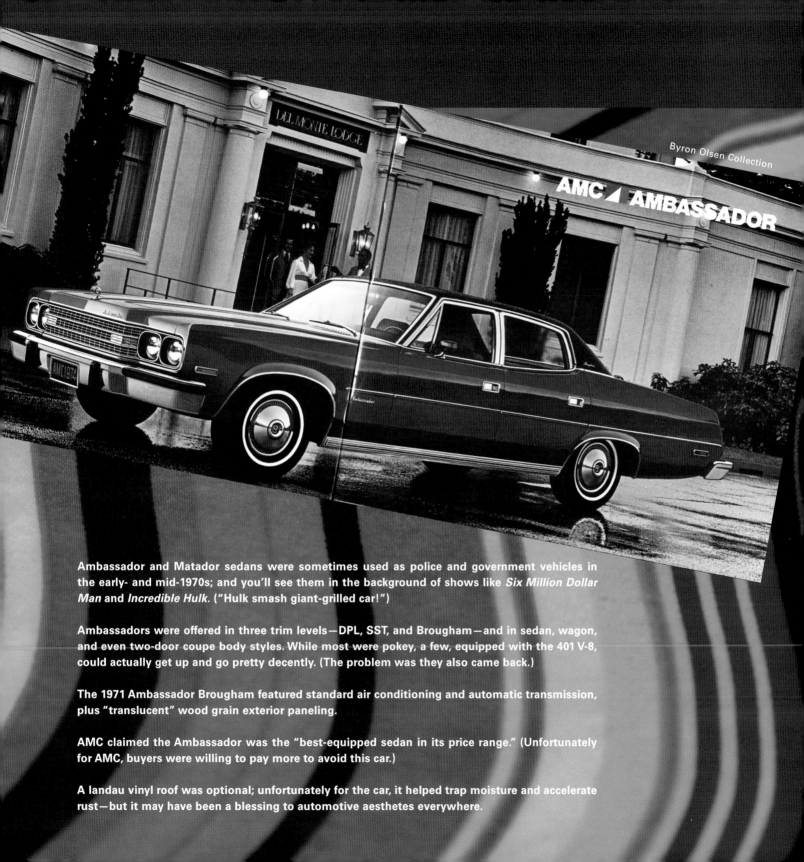

DEL MONTE LODGE

AMC ◢ AMBASSADOR

Ambassador and Matador sedans were sometimes used as police and government vehicles in the early- and mid-1970s; and you'll see them in the background of shows like *Six Million Dollar Man* and *Incredible Hulk*. ("Hulk smash giant-grilled car!")

Ambassadors were offered in three trim levels—DPL, SST, and Brougham—and in sedan, wagon, and even two-door coupe body styles. While most were pokey, a few, equipped with the 401 V-8, could actually get up and go pretty decently. (The problem was they also came back.)

The 1971 Ambassador Brougham featured standard air conditioning and automatic transmission, plus "translucent" wood grain exterior paneling.

AMC claimed the Ambassador was the "best-equipped sedan in its price range." (Unfortunately for AMC, buyers were willing to pay more to avoid this car.)

A landau vinyl roof was optional; unfortunately for the car, it helped trap moisture and accelerate rust—but it may have been a blessing to automotive aesthetes everywhere.

Dishonorable
Mentions

National Automotive History Collection

1979 Mercedes-Benz 300D

Few experiences compare with driving an expensive luxury car so slow it can barely make it to 60 miles per hour in less than 20 seconds (19.3 seconds to be precise), the "Monty Burns" standard for pitiful acceleration. When new, the 300D retailed for nearly $30,000—an impressive stack of bills 25 years ago—especially for a car that couldn't outrun a VW hippy van. Its five-cylinder diesel engine developed just 88 horsepower (125, if you ordered the optional turbocharger) to deal with the hulk of nearly 4,000 pounds of lead sled Mercedes. But it was an improvement over its predecessor, the 240D, which needed even more time to reach 60 and topped out around 85 with a tailwind.

DRESS SUITS TO RENT

1987 Zimmer Golden Spirit

Famous—or infamous—for its retro-1930s-style roadsters, the Zimmer Motor Golden Spirit may have looked like a Duesenberg SJ at a distance, but under the skin it was just a custom-bodied Buick Regal, the high-end equivalent of those converted Volkswagen Beetles you used to see outfitted with Rolls-Royce grilles. Zimmer Motor Car Company ceased to exist after 1987, although an unrelated "Zimmer"—Art Zimmer of Syracuse, New York—revived the cars in 1997 with the Art Zimmer Neo-Classic Motor Car Company. (Another low-volume manufacturer of latter day "classics"—Excalibur Motors—joined Zimmer on the scrap heap of automotive history just five years later.)

1988 Buick Reatta

Basically an over-glitzed and chopped-down Riviera, this two-seat coupe was one of several abortive attempts by Buick to jazz up the product line—and hopefully, draw in a buyer less like Bob Dole and more like Mel Gibson. The Reatta featured a 165-horsepower 3.8-liter V-6 and front-wheel drive, as well as a stupendous $35,000 price tag. In 1990, a convertible version was offered, but fewer than 3,000 were sold. Total production of this automotive belly flop never topped 22,000 units over its three-year run.

National Automotive History Collection

124

Thunderbird with Exterior Luxury Group in Pastel Sand (6D) with matching vinyl roof

Spread your wings.

There have been many exciting, innovative Thunderbirds over the past 25 years and the 1980 model is destined to be another. If this is your year to become a new Thunderbird owner, you have chosen the greatest year yet to "spread your wings."

Exterior Luxury Group, seen here, features: opera windows, padded rear half vinyl roof, center pillar wraparound appliqué, vinyl insert bodyside moldings, bodyside paint stripes, dual remote control mirrors, and luxury wheel covers (wire wheel covers shown). Interior Luxury Group also shown.

For Standard Features, see page 13. Some items shown are optional. See pages 16–19 for detailed options listing.

Your dealer has actual samples of colors and trims coded by letter in the text.

Byron Olsen Collection

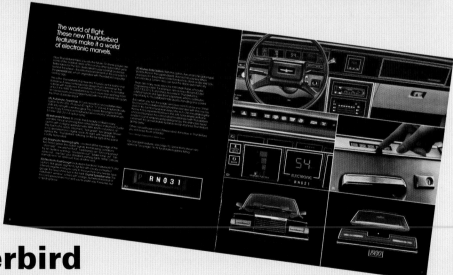

1980 Ford Thunderbird

What began as a sexy Corvette competitor in the mid-1950s and evolved into a high-class, four-seat boulevardier by the 1970s had become by 1980 a landau-roofed, overstuffed (and overpriced) Ford Fairmont. The 1979 T-Bird was still a presentable car—not an obvious fraud like the 1980, which had only its tail-lights, grille, and the vinyl on the roof to distinguish it from the donor car it was based upon. Buyers responded appropriately and sales tanked by almost 200,000 units compared to the 1978–1979 model year.

1985 Cadillac DeVille

This was the first year for the "all new" and front-wheel-drive, "downsized" DeVille (and Fleetwood), formerly Cadillac's largest and most impressive sedans. It wasn't so much that the car was physically smaller—it was that it still tried to look big, creating a weirdly dysmorphic ensemble that resulted in a massive decline in sales of almost 20,000 units over the previous year. GM also charged you more for less car. The 1985 DeVille carried an MSRP of $18,571, almost $1,000 more than the larger, more powerful, and still dignified 1984 model.

National Automotive History Collection

1984 Peugeot 505

A true road toad with 96 horsepower and just 2 liters under the hood, the 505 was slower than Oprah running up a flight of stairs—while carrying Dr. Phil—and could be recognized by the furrowed brow of its gloomy-looking front end and the rheumy gaze of its quick-to-yellow headlight covers. The 505's headlights also leaked—and would sometimes accumulate an inch or three of water, which sloshed around incontinently like a liquored-up roué by the banks of the River Seine. A smelly 76-horsepower diesel version was available that required 18 seconds to reach 60 miles per hour—neck and neck with mimes on mopeds. Beret optional.

Just when you thought it was safe to go back to the car dealer . . .

The Pontiac Aztek

The only vehicle to look like it's been in a bad accident even before it left the factory, the Aztek will be remembered as evidence that advanced degrees in automotive design are not necessarily indicators of good taste—or spelling ability. What's truly remarkable about the Aztek, however, is not its revolting appearance. Rather, it is that it was built by General Motors—an enormous automotive combine in which no decision is made without being pored over by a small army of middle managers, product planners, and senior executives. There are many people to blame for this case of automotive food poisoning, not just a "lone nut," as could be said of AMC.

Initial sales of the Aztek were so poor that GM reportedly insisted that middle managers drive them as company cars—in order to give the impression that people were buying them.

The projected first-year production of 75,000 units was just a little off the mark. As the first year drew to a close, fewer than 10,000 Azteks had been purchased by non-fleet (rental car) buyers.

How lame is it that GM thought misspelling "Aztec" would make this malformed car cool?